Mind the Gap: Your Taxes

Tax for Teens, Young Adults, and Travellers

Tyler from Perth

Copyright © 2018 Tyler Jenkins

All rights reserved.

ISBN: 0648273105
ISBN-13: 978-0648273103

CONTENTS

Introduction — Pg 5

Chapter One – What is Tax? — Pg 21

Chapter Two – What is the ATO? — Pg 27

Chapter Three – What is a Financial Year? — Pg 32

Chapter Four – What is a Tax File Number? — Pg 40

Chapter Five – What are the Financial Documents? — Pg 48

Chapter Six – What is Tax Withholding? — Pg 56

Chapter Seven – What is a TFN Declaration? — Pg 62

Chapter Eight – What is a PAYG Payment Summary? — Pg 71

Chapter Nine – What are Deductions? — Pg 78

Chapter Ten – What is a Tax Return? — Pg 85

Chapter Eleven – What is a Tax Agent? — Pg 96

Chapter Twelve – What is MyTax? — Pg 105

Chapter Thirteen – What is a Tax Assessment? — Pg 112

Chapter Fourteen – How Can I Stay Organised? — Pg 118

Chapter Fifteen – How Can I Save Money? — Pg 125

Chapter Sixteen – Tax for Travellers — Pg 130

Extra Information — Pg 137

Final Quiz — Pg 139

Thank You and Answers — Pg 143

Index of Terms — Pg 148

A special thanks goes to Nick Wactor,
    A meticulous editor, design advisor, and moral support.

Welcome to the World of *Mind the Gap*!

There are some basics about tax and money that we all need here in Australia. Sadly, few of these skills are taught in our school system. This is your personal handbook on those very skills.

Let me show you what this book can do for you.

What's the Problem?
Just imagine that there were hundreds of millions of dollars up for grabs.
Hoards of cash, left unclaimed by their rightful owners, just sitting in a government bank account waiting for people to get their act together and claim it.

That's the situation right now, as you're reading this.

Every year, multitudes of people "forget" to lodge their returns.
Their refunds? Pfft, just sitting around with inflation eating at them.
Your average teenager (and heck, even a huge proportion of adults) might not lodge for four, five, six years straight. I saw it as teacher: my students were making these mistakes, of course. But then I realised – even my fellow teachers didn't have it together.

Then there's the lost money in deductions, the interest rates and charges for underpaid taxes, and the volumes of cash swindled by the dishonest every year...
Should I go on?

And what does it take to get it right?
We have young adults and seasoned workers alike scratching their heads when they're asked about "attributed personal-services income" and "self-education expenses".

Teens as young as 14 can get a job in Australia.
Then it's not long before the ATO is asking them about deductable expenses, fringe benefits, and voluntary super contributions.

There's something missing from the education system. Am I right?

So, What is *Mind the Gap?*

Mind the Gap is an Australian business that educates Australia's newest young workers on how to survive 'out there.' *Mind the Gap* offers books, an online course of study and resource centre, and tactile student workshops in schools across our country.

There is a gap in our education system, and *Mind the Gap* was designed to be your bridge.

Mind the Gap is Australian-owned and founded. It was created by an everyday guy just like you. Tyler (from Perth) wanted to make life easier for the next generation of workers.

Who is Tyler from Perth?
Tyler from Perth (AKA Tyler Jenkins) is a real person as well as a character in the coming chapters. He's the author of this book and the founder of *Mind the Gap*.

Tyler has a degree in commerce and transcontinental experience as an educator. He's taught a tertiary-level business and worked in several educational, charitable, and developmental programs in Europe, Asia and the United States.

Who is Hayden Hayes?
Hayden Hayes is a fictional character, and he asks just about any question that could be asked. He's sixteen, and has just got his first job! See his introduction later on in this chapter.

Who should buy this book?
This book was written to benefit everyone working in the Australian workforce. It aims to simplify the stuff no one wants to care about, but everyone has to deal with. Some people who could use this book:
1) Teenagers.
2) Teachers looking to bridge the gap in their education program.
3) Parents, who know their children need to start with their best foot forward.
4) People arriving in Australia from other nations.
5) Adults who know they're missing some of the basics.

Why was this book written?
When I left high school, I was embarrassed. Embarrassed for me and embarrassed for my school. I could draw the structure of a complex carbon atom, recite Shakespeare, construct (to a lesser degree) technical mathematics, and recount the controversies of Australian history in a global context.

But I didn't know what a tax return was.

Or when it was due.
Or how to complete it.
Or where to go for help.
I didn't know how to take steps to secure myself from the most basic financial follies.

I got my first job, and I felt the fool. I stared blank-faced at an exasperated employer, TFN declaration and superannuation choice forms in his hand, as I admitted I had no idea what any of these things were.
Yes, I felt embarrassed. But it wasn't my fault.

This book and program is here to offer Australia's youth what they've needed all along. It's here to teach them how to 'adult'.

After all, wasn't that the point of education?

Introductory Quiz!

Test Yourself! How much do you know about adulting in Australia?

1. PAYG Withholding Tax is:
    a. The method of paying income tax – "Pay as you go", or "pay as you earn".
    b. A type of income tax called "Payers Australia Yearly Gains".
    c. A category "G" Payment, where you take the money from your pay check and give it to the tax office every quarter.
    d. Payments that are held by the tax office, as a penalty for not paying taxes.
    e. A way to withhold tax from the government until you are ready to pay it.
2. You must complete your tax return:
    a. At the end of the calendar year.
    b. By Halloween.
    c. Just before the end of the financial year – the end of the financial year is the deadline.
    d. Just before the end of the calendar year – the end of the calendar year is the deadline.
    e. The ATO will inform you of your due date – it's different for each employee.
3. A tax file number is:
    a. The file at the tax office which holds the tax information for your family.
    b. A personal identifier – a number that identifies you to the Tax Office.
    c. The number allocated to each tax return as it is submitted (different for each tax return).
    d. All of the above
4. A good time to get your tax file number is:
    a. At least 30 days before you get your first job – it's impossible to work without a tax file number.
    b. You get your first job or before – as soon as you can (it's in your best interests).
    c. One floats down from the sky, because life is that easy.
    d. As late as you can, so you don't have to pay taxes for ages.
    e. Every person is automatically given a TFN.
5. A tax return is:
    a. When you have to return money to the government, because you didn't pay enough taxes.

b. The amount of money the government returns to you for paying too much tax during the year.
   c. A form you fill out to help the tax office do a final tax count for the year just passed.
   d. The money you get when your tax assessment is returned to you.
   e. A document you fill out usually in December.
6. If you pay too much in withholding:
   a. You don't get it back.
   b. You should file a standard over-withholding form with the ATO to get your money back.
   c. You can't pay too much in withholding. The ATO is too careful and takes exactly the correct amount each time.
   d. It'll be returned to you when you lodge a tax return for that year.
   e. You have to file for a tax amendment.
7. An employee's income taxes are generally paid:
   a. By cash or card at any ATO shop front.
   b. By deducting the money directly from a person's pay.
   c. In the same way electricity or water bills are paid – a bill is sent.
   d. Whichever way of the above you choose to pay.
   e. At the end of the year with a tax return.
8. Forgetting to list a tax deduction will cause:
   a. You to get a smaller tax refund.
   b. You to pay more taxes throughout the year.
   c. You to get in trouble with the ATO, even fined.
   d. Nothing, tax deductions are withheld automatically.
9. What is a tax deduction?
   a. A reduction in the amount of tax you pay because of your living conditions.
   b. An expense – something you bought that you needed specifically for work. It means you pay less tax.
   c. The tax deducted from your pay check and sent to the ATO as withholding taxes.
   d. A voluntary payment of your taxes, paid as you buy something at a store, instead of paying the taxes through your employer.
10. A tax return is used by:
    a. The ATO, to produce a PAYG payment summary and therefore a potential refund.
    b. Your boss, to pay your taxes to the ATO.
    c. The ATO, to produce a tax assessment and therefore a potential refund.

d. You, it's the money you get back from the ATO.

e. The ATO, because they can't give you your weekly wages without it.

11. What is a tax agent?

    a. Someone who organises your tax withholding.

    b. Someone who prepares your tax assessment.

    c. Someone who prepares your tax return.

    d. All of the above.

Answers!

1) A
2) B
3) B
4) B
5) C
6) D
7) B
8) A
9) B
10) C
11) C

How were your results?

Case Studies

Toby
Early 20s

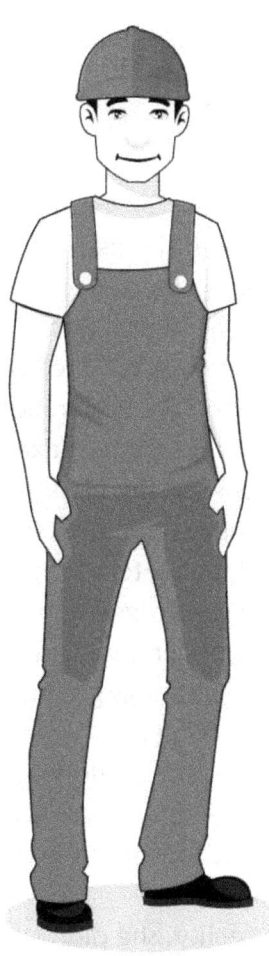

Toby didn't really care too much about all this stuff, so long as he had a good hourly wage and was paid on time: the rest seemed to sort itself out. At first, he wasn't doing a lot of hours, but when he finished school those hours increased. No one picked up that he had incorrectly not claimed the tax free threshold, so he was paying a lot more in tax each and every week than he should be.

Life was pretty hectic, and like it didn't really click for the first couple of years that he should be filing tax returns. One day, as the end of the financial year approached, he got his act together. He filed three tax returns at once, and Toby got the best news ever - the payout was huge! He was due a tax refund of $2000 a year for three years – it was better than Christmas!

But then the truth sank in a little bit. He got the cash, but the delay had cost him.

Inflation had gotten to his money, and the payout of $6000 (had it been accumulating interest in a bank account for that time) could have earned him another $749. Not only that, his brothers had just bought a home together. Toby wasn't able to save enough to join them. That payout of almost $7000 could have made the difference: he might have been a home owner.

Refund with applied interest rate of six percent:

2020	2021	2022	2023
$2000	$2120	$2247	$2382
	$2000	$2120	$2247
		$2000	$2120
		Total	$6749

Heather
Mid 20s

Heather had the opposite problem to Toby. Heather worked several jobs at the same time, and claimed the tax-free threshold for each one. It seemed like the logical thing to do – why pay tax when you don't have to? She also didn't declare her HECS debt on for TFN declaration form.
Easy mistake to make when you're not thinking. But when she filed her return, she owed a lot of money to the tax office - $4000! For one year! It was bad timing too – she was moving house and was already struggling to meet the expenses of the move. It took her a while to pay it all back.
Finally, things got back to normal before she realised something else. In her industry and her position, there were a lot of work-related expenses she'd missed. Her fellow co-workers had been claiming things in deductions that she didn't know she was allowed to claim.
In reality, she didn't even know what it meant to claim deductions at all.

Heather started keeping her receipts so that she could do things differently this year.

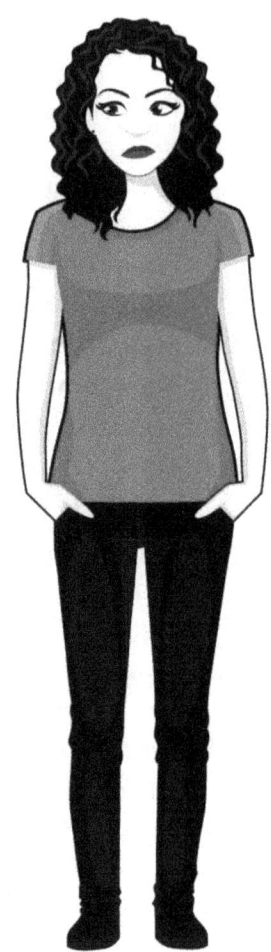

Liz
Mid 20s

Liz figured she was doing the right thing. Her friend had a mate that was good with taxes, and she saved money on a tax agent by getting him to lodge her return. She didn't know much about this stuff, but her refund seemed nice each year so she didn't question it.

One day the ATO approached her asking for some documented proof of her deductions, as they were higher than others in her industry. This was the first time she actually looked at her tax situation, and that's when she realised something wasn't quite right.

That friend of a friend, who then seemed then to have disappeared back to his hometown overseas, had been making big claims and pocketing the difference. Now, Elizabeth was looking down the barrel of the ATO with some questions to answer.

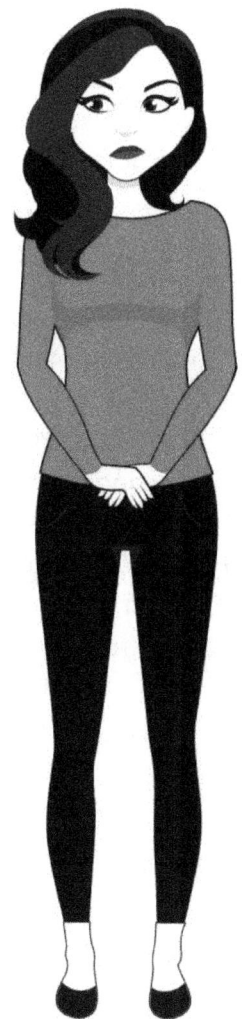

These situations are just examples: the three characters above are not real people. However, they are based on real stories. These things really do happen, and they happen all the time.

It doesn't take much to avoid strife – just take a few knowledgeable precautions.

How can I use this book?

This book is designed to be a giant frequently-asked-questions pamphlet. All information is sorted by question: just about anything you could ask, with real life examples.

The anatomy of each chapter:
1) The Problem – Hayden's Problem.
2) Why do I need to know this?
3) Key info – a brief summary for impatient readers.
4) Answering your questions – typical questions that are asked.
5) Tips and Tricks – how to come out a winner in each situation.
6) Hayden's solution
7) Key terms
8) Quiz

Introducing: Hayden Hayes!

Right, so...
PAYG summaries, TFN declarations, tax assessments...
Yep. Someone wanna give me a headstart?

Hayden's sixteen years old.
He's just been hired at a local store: his first ever job.
Like many teenagers, no one gave him the run-down of the boring stuff.

Hayden doesn't earn a lot yet, but he works hard for his money. It's that hard-earned money that's on the line: thousands of people every year lose money and time because they weren't given the tools to look out for themselves.

That's where *Mind the Gap* comes into the story. Follow along as Hayden and Tyler figure out all the important stuff throughout the whole financial year.

His circumstances might not be all that different from yours. See how he saves himself the time and money that many people in Aussie history have lost.

Introducing: Tyler from Perth!

There's some stuff that you might need to know when you start work.

Tyler guides Hayden through the financial year, step by step.

He's here to answer questions.

Introducing the Rest of the Crew!

Hayden's Boss
The guy who pays Hayden's pay check. He sure looks wealthy, right? It's actually not an altogether fair representation – many business owners really struggle.

Hayden's Tax Agent
Hayden's tax defender! The accountant that gives him advice, helps him file his returns, and, well, is just an all-round nice person.

The Tax Man
The tax man himself.
He's not a bad guy, but unfortunately for him, usually no one talks about him unless something bad is happening.

This book contains general advice only, and does not take into account your personal situation. *Mind the Gap* recommends the services of a tax professional.

Chapter One: What is tax?

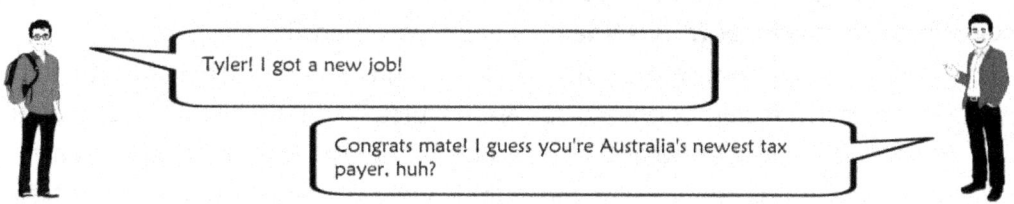

Why do I need this chapter?
You need this chapter to understand the *what* and *why* of tax.
1) What is tax?
2) Why do we have to pay it at all?
3) Who has to pay tax?
4) What kinds of tax are important for me?
5) What happens if I don't pay tax?
6) What happens if I don't understand tax at all?

What is Tax?
Tax is when the government takes some of our wages to pay for the costs of running the country. Why? To keep our country beautiful, functioning, and safe.

What does my tax money pay for?
Taxes pay for many things:
- ✓ Roads
- ✓ Hospitals
- ✓ Schools
- ✓ Police
- ✓ Firemen
- ✓ Ambulances
- ✓ National Defence
- ✓ Public Infrastructure
- ✓ Libraries
- ✓ Parks
- ✓ Beaches
- ✓ Other stuff too

Who has to pay taxes?
Generally, every working person in Australia has to pay taxes, it doesn't matter how old you are, where you live, or which job you do. The amount of tax will change though. If you earn only a small amount in a year, for example, you may not have to pay income tax for that year.

What are some different types of taxes?
Some types of tax for the average person:
1) **Income tax** (this is a tax on what you earn)
    We'll come back to this important one in a second!
2) **Goods and Service tax** (this is a tax on what you spend)
    When you pay stuff, almost anything, you have to pay 10% extra to the government. It's a tax on "goods and services". A good or service could be anything! It includes buying a meal in a restaurant, a pair of shoes in a shop, or a car-washing service at a carwash. If you've been shopping in Australia, you're guaranteed to have paid this one already.
3) **Property Taxes** (this is a tax on owning a house)
    There are different types of these.
    Stamp Duty, for example, happens when you sell a house. It's a fee to the government for organising the paperwork to show the change of the owner. Did you know? The government keeps records of who owns which house! When you want to change the owner, you have to pay a fee for record-keeping.
    Then there might be land taxes too. It depends which state you live in!
4) **The Medicare Levy** – a tax to pay for public healthcare!

These are just some examples. There are also many other taxes for businesses.

Speed this up for me – what do I need to know about?
Income tax is the most important one for someone to understand when they start working. It's also called PAYG tax. That's what we focus on in this book.
This book is organised as an series of frequently asked questions – skip to the bit you need!

What's PAYG Tax?
It's another name for income tax.
When they say "PAYG", they're talking about how often you pay income tax – "Pay As You Go". The idea is that as you earn money, a little bit of that money goes to the government. Each time you get paid, you pay the tax at the same time. A lot of the time, your boss will do all the paper work for you, so you'll barely even notice.

What kind of problems might I have with tax, if I don't understand what I'm doing?
Here are just some possible problems you might have with tax if you aren't careful:
   1) You lose money (eg, your refund is smaller than it should be).
   2) You don't pay your taxes (you end up with a bill or worse).

3) You're late with your returns (you risk fines and delay your refund, losing potential interest).
4) You file your paperwork wrong (and cause more issues for yourself, including owing money and/or getting into trouble).
5) You lose or misunderstand important paperwork (again, just making more problems for yourself, especially in the long-run).
6) You spend 10 hours doing something wrong that you could've done right by lunch time.

How do people accidentally pay too much tax?
This is actually a pretty common mistake, and people don't even know they make it! It's your responsibility to be careful with your tax returns, get good advice, and minimize your taxes. No one from the government will help you pay less tax: they will actually let you pay too much, without blinking an eye! A good tax accountant can help you with this, and this book will give you some pointers too.

What happens if I don't pay tax?
This is actually quite hard to do if you're an employee. Even if you're intent on breaking the law and evading tax, your boss (who controls your pay) will take some money and pay the tax automatically. It'll happen without you even noticing.

If you do find a way not to pay it, however, (this is more possible if you run your own business) you could get into big trouble. Some people have been sent to prison for tax evasion. They also have to pay the tax back with interest and fines! So be careful. You need to know what forms you're filling out, and how to do it properly. You don't want to accidentally evade your taxes.
Seriously though, you don't.
I've heard some stories, man.

What happens when I'm late with my tax return?
The simple answer is that if you don't file your tax return on time, you could get fined. More commonly, you miss out on a lot of money in your tax refund until you do file it.
See the chapters about filing your tax return and the financial year for information on tax returns and deadlines.

Why do so many people waste so much time and get so frustrated with taxes?
Taxes are hard. They're hard, and they're boring. They're hard because they're boring. People get annoyed and they don't know where to go for good help. Luckily for you, you have this book and the *Mind the Gap* website. That's a good

start. That, and a really good accountant (see the chapter on accountants), will keep you knowledgeable and safe, and make your life a lot easier.

Tips and Tricks!
Some places to go to for help:
1) An accountant/tax agent.
2) The Australian Tax Office website and phone line.
3) The *Mind the Gap* book and website.

You can also try these (be careful! These are not always accurate!):
1) Family and friends.
2) General internet searches.
3) Your boss.

Update from Hayden:
Hayden just got his first part time job. He didn't know anything about taxes yet, so he's done a few things to learn about how the system works.
1) He talked to his parents and they suggested some great steps to take.
2) Now's he's reading *Mind the Gap,* and doing the online course.
3) His boss gave him some forms to fill out. He had a question about his taxes, so he called the tax office early in the morning and asked them all the questions he could think of.
4) He wrote down the name of his father's tax accountant, and he'll use him to file his tax return when the time comes!

Important Key Ideas!
1) Tax — Money to the government to pay for our country.
2) Income tax — A tax on what we earn.
3) PAYG tax — A different name for income tax: Pay As You Go tax.
4) Tax accountant/agent — Someone who helps you with your taxes.
5) Australian Tax Office — The government office for taxes.
6) Tax Evasion — Not paying your taxes.
7) GST — Goods and services tax, a tax on what you buy.

CHAPTER ONE QUIZ TIME!

Link these ideas to their names!
1) PAYG Tax
2) Tax Accountant/Tax Agent
3) Australian Tax Office
4) Tax Evasion
5) GST
6) Stamp Duty

A) The government office for taxes
B) A tax on selling a house
C) Pay As You Go income tax.
D) The act of not paying your taxes.
E) Someone who helps you with your taxes.
F) A tax on what you buy.

7) Income tax is:
   a. The name given to all types of tax because this is the government's "income".
   b. A tax on what a person earns as income during the financial year.
   c. A tax on employers hiring employees.
   d. The only tax that will affect the average person.
8) PAYG Withholding Tax is:
   a. The method of paying income tax – "Pay as you go", or "pay as you earn".
   b. A type of income tax called "Payers Australia Yearly Gains".
   c. A category "G" Payment, where you take the money from your pay check and give it to the tax office every quarter.
   d. Payments that are held by the tax office, as a penalty for not paying taxes.
   e. A way to withhold tax from the government until you are ready to pay it.
9) Income tax is the most important tax for the average person to understand because:
   a. It affects just about everyone.
   b. It requires you to do some paperwork after each financial year.
   c. It is often the primary form of tax payment for Australian workers.
   d. All of the above.
10) You pay income tax:
    a. At the end of the financial year.
    b. At the beginning of the financial year.
    c. As you earn it – paid from each pay check.
    d. Whenever you get a chance.

11) Taxation is:
    a. Is in place so that Australia can pay for public infrastructure and other stuff the government provides.
    b. Always simple and easy to understand.
    c. Something you don't need to worry about until you're 18 years old.
    d. Is not strictly enforced on teenagers.
    e. All of the above.
12) There are taxes on:
    a. What you earn, what you buy, sometimes things you own or use.
    b. What you earn, what you spend, and who you vote for.
    c. What you spend, what you earn, and who you live with.
    d. What you do, where you go, and what you wear.
13) Tax is something:
    a. I need to be an expert in before I become an adult.
    b. Easy and doesn't require expertise.
    c. That will be made easier if I seek help from an expert.
    d. That I MUST, by law, seek out help with from a qualified expert.
14) It's good to know the basics about tax because:
    a. You will be faced with tax all your life.
    b. You can then give your friends financial advice.
    c. Because it's so very interesting.
    d. It's not good to know about tax. I'm putting my fingers in my ears, singing "la la la," and not filing a single tax return for the next 40 years.

Chapter Two:
What is the Australian Tax Office?

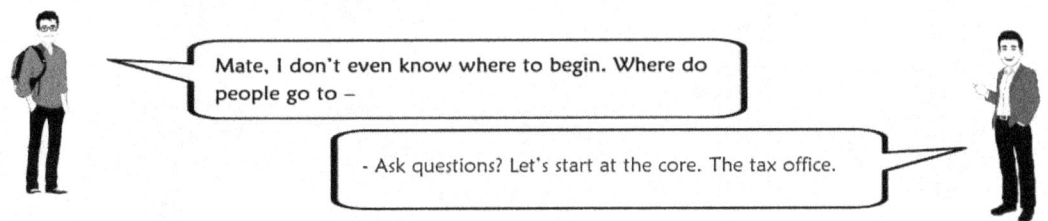

Mate, I don't even know where to begin. Where do people go to –

- Ask questions? Let's start at the core. The tax office.

Why do I need this chapter?
This chapter explains *who* and *where* of the government tax office.
1) Who do I talk to about this tax stuff? Who's in charge here?
2) Where are they?
3) Who will chase me for things that are late?
4) Who will come after me if I do the wrong thing?

What is the ATO?
The Australian Tax Office (ATO) is the government agency that collects and administers taxes for Australia.

Who or what is the ATO?
As I'm sure you know, but the government is pretty big – there's lots of stuff going on. That's a lot of different people and departments doing lots of different tasks. One department of the government is called the ATO: **the Australian Tax Office**. Collecting, calculating and checking Australia's taxes is the responsibility of these guys.

What do they do?
They're pretty useful. These are the people you talk to when you submit a tax return, or when you have a problem. Try to always do the right thing by the tax office, because it's very easy to get in some trouble, either for deliberately doing the wrong thing, or for just being lazy.
Yes, we get busy. But it's important to know: with taxes, falling behind can get you into trouble. You have obligations as an Australian citizen to pay your taxes and maintain your records with the ATO. If you don't, someone from the ATO might come to investigate you.

How do I get in touch with the ATO?
Let's pretend for a moment that you have a question for the tax office about your tax situation:
1) They have a website with plenty of information: www.ato.gov.au
2) Most people call the ATO with their questions (you can find their phone number on their site).
3) Your tax agent can chat with them for you.

Why chat with the ATO?
Maybe you have a problem with your tax return.
Or a question about the withholding rates.
Maybe you're filing your return yourself: some people don't want an accountant. They want to do the whole process themselves. Those people often use the ATO's resources a lot – their website, their call centre, and their information booklets. If you have a question about tax, the ATO is one place you can go to for help. If it's something you really don't know much about, you could ask a more experienced friend first, but be careful! They may not always be correct.

Am I supposed to know this stuff already?
Nope. In the past, people weren't really taught this stuff. And no one really knows it all. There are people in their 30s, 40s, and 50s who still don't get the basic ideas, because no one taught them! Lucky for you – you're now a step ahead.

If you're anything like me when I did my first taxes, you might walk away from the accountant's office or get off the phone with the ATO more confused than when you started, and you'll have no idea what to do next. There is a lot to understand. Always have a list of questions, and power through them! That's how you'll end up wiser than your friends.

Tips and Tricks
1) Use the resources the ATO provides!
   a. The ATO's fact sheets, Tax Help, and online stuff.
   b. The ATO phone line.
2) You've got *Mind the Gap*'s online learning stuff too.
3) Don't be afraid to ask stupid questions.

The ATO publishes lots of stuff on the internet to help you. Their fact sheets are full of information if you like reading. They also send out information and advice via social media, and that includes some videos on YouTube that explain how things work.

They also have something called *Tax Help*. It's for people who don't earn much and need help filing their tax returns. It's free, and they can show you how to file your tax returns online. Don't forget you can call them as well! The early morning is the best time, before they're busy.

Update from Hayden:
Hayden wasn't great with this stuff, so he...
1) Made a list of questions and called the ATO.
2) Talked to his parents.
3) Asked his boss.

There was lots of stuff online, but he didn't like reading, so he...
4) watched a video or two from *Mind the Gap* and then the ATO's YouTube channel.

Important Key Ideas!
1) ATO — Australian Tax Office
2) Tax Help — A Free Tax Service for Low-Income Earners
3) ATO Fact Sheets — Information Sheets from the ATO about Different Topics

CHAPTER TWO QUIZ TIME!
1. What does "ATO" stand for?

2. Name three things the ATO does to help you with your taxes.

3. Why does the tax office exist? What does it do?

Choose the correct answer!
4. The Australian Tax Office:
    a. Administers (follows up on) taxation on behalf of the government.
    b. Writes up new tax legislation for the government.
    c. Is not contactable unless you are the government.
    d. All of the above
5. The Tax Office (and it's tools and resources):
    a. Is not a good place to go for help.
    b. Is often a good place to go for help (as is a tax specialist, and perhaps your parents).
    c. Will not help the general public.
6. The best way to solve a tax problem is to:
    a. Write down all your questions and talk to the ATO.
    b. Write down all your questions and talk to your tax agent.
    c. Use good online resources like the ATO's YouTube channel and *Mind the Gap*.
    d. All of the above. When one doesn't answer the question fully, seek a second and third opinion.
7. The ATO is the organisation I can use to:
    a. Submit a tax return.
    b. Apply for a tax file number.
    c. Learn about my tax obligations.
    d. All the above.
8. Being lazy is dangerous with the ATO because:
    a. There are deadlines you are responsible for, as an Australian citizen.
    b. They can ease the tax burden on people they think are more responsible.
    c. As a citizen, you can be kicked out of Australia for not paying your taxes.
    d. It's fine to be lazy. My friend Larry is lazy and he's doing great.
9. The ATO:
    a. Is open 24-hours a day so that you can pay your taxes.
    b. Is not available to help you with any problems you have.

c. Can answer your questions, but is not an education program, and therefore is limited in how much time it can offer in explaining taxation to young people.
d. Is no use to anyone.

Chapter Three:
What is a Financial Year?

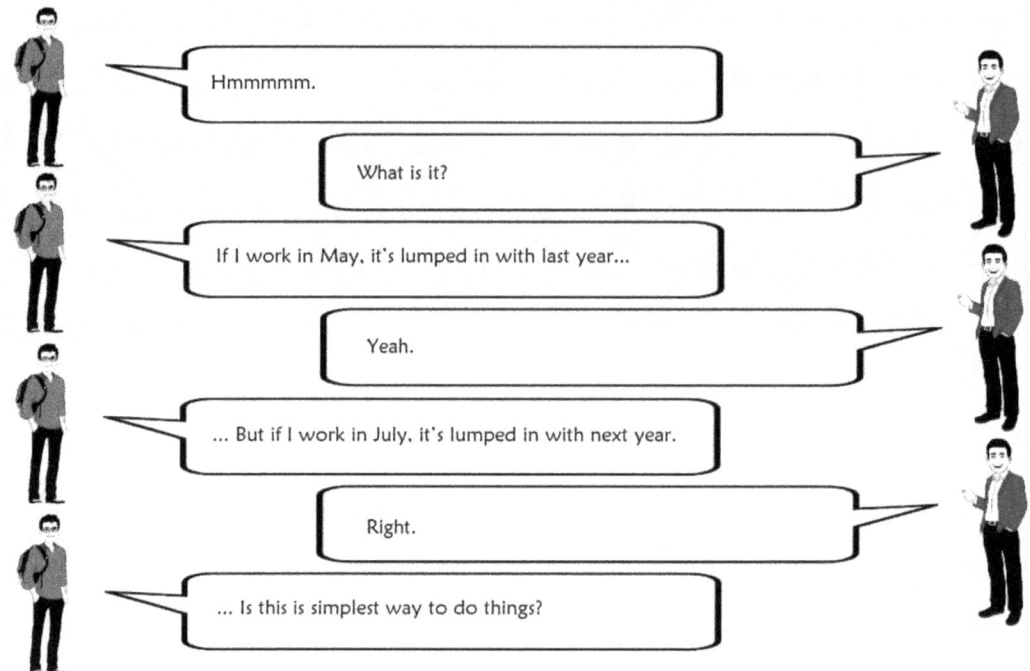

Why do I need this chapter?
This chapter explains the *when* of taxes.
1) When is my tax return due?
2) What is a financial year and why is it different?
3) How does the financial year affect me?

What is the Financial Year?
The financial year is the calendar for finances and business. It starts and ends on different dates compared to the normal calendar year.

What's the difference between a calendar year and a financial year?
One's for the financial world, and the other is for everything else.
The both have a specific beginning and end.
They're both 12 months long.
They both have all the usual months of the year: January, July and December.
They're just used for different purposes.

Why are they different?
Let's say you're a businessman. When the normal year ends in December, can you imagine everyone trying to do their paperwork? Figuring out their profits for the year, doing their taxes, figuring out stock... When the year ends, the business world is busy finishing all the business books for the year.
If you're a businessman or accountant, or anyone in the business world, this is the busiest time. There's so much to do.

But what are you normally doing at the end of the year?
It's Christmas!
Bad Timing. So, they changed the system to make it easier for workers and businesses.

When does the financial year start and end?
The financial year ends at the end of June, on June 30th, and the new year begins the next day on July 1st. It's still exactly 12 months like a normal year.

For business, the year ends exactly 6-months after the holiday period, and as far away from the holiday period as possible.

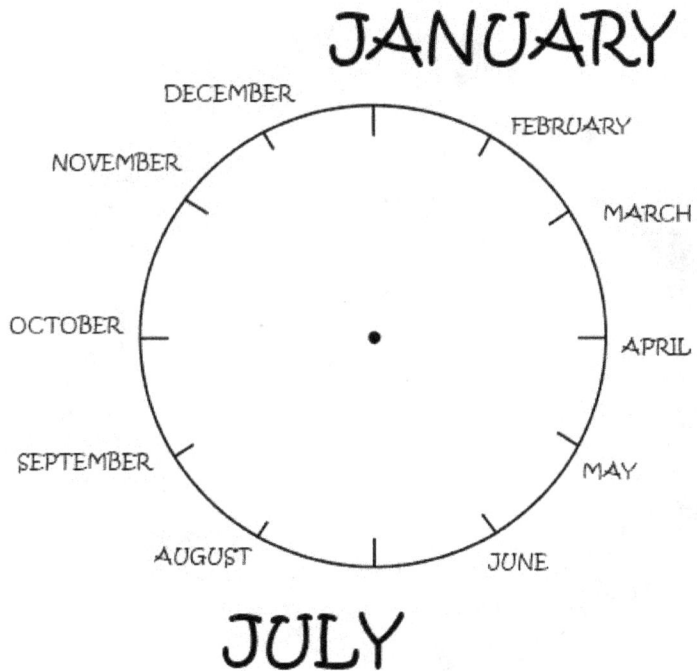

The government and tax office chose this date to begin the financial year for taxes and businesses in Australia. It meant that the end of year paperwork could be done during the middle of the year, when no one's on holidays and all staff are available to work.

Though it might be a little confusing at first, the financial year was an invention to make the business world run smoother.

Is it the same for everyone?
Different countries have different financial years, and some businesses and companies in Australia even choose their financial year to suit their business. That's allowed!

What does this mean for you?
Whatever job you work, you're working in the business world, and you have to pay your taxes. All of your individual tax paperwork is due according to the financial year.

When is my tax return due?
(For information on what a tax return is, see chapter the tax return chapter)
Between July 1st and October 31st is your 4-month window to complete tax returns. After that date, your return would be overdue.

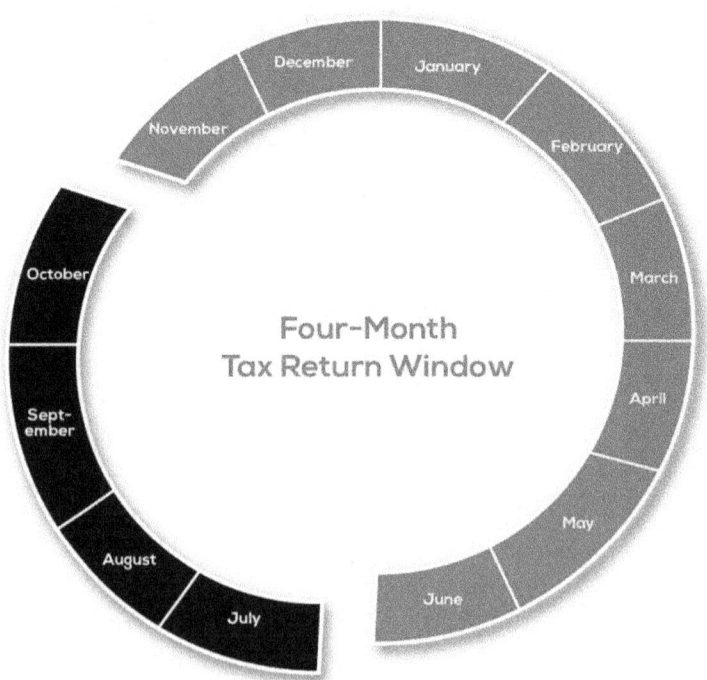

What name do we give to each financial year?

So, if half of this financial year belongs to one calendar year, and the other half belongs to another calendar year, how do we identify the financial years? What do we call them?

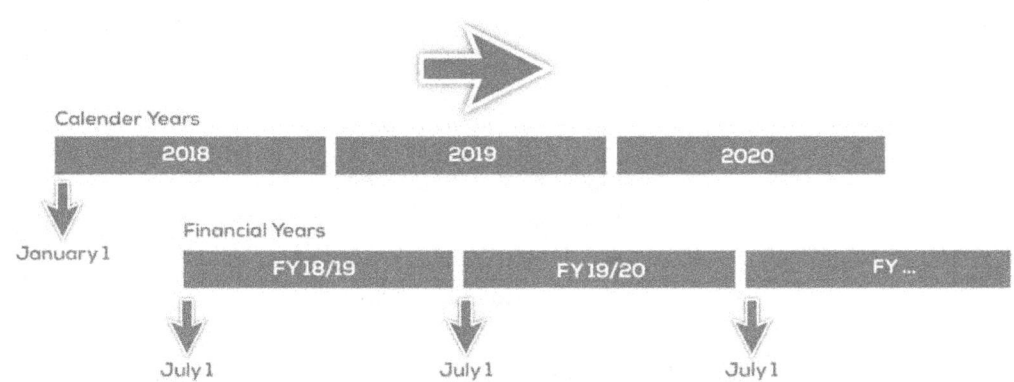

Generally we refer to financial years in one of two ways:

We often name them by the year in which it ends. The financial year half in 2019 and half in 2020 would be called **the year ending 2020**.

The other option is to simply call it **the financial year 19/20**, with a slash dividing the years.

Tips and Tricks!
1) Put a reminder in your calendar or phone for the end of the financial year, to remind you to collect your paperwork from your boss and do your return. Don't forget! The due date is Halloween!
2) For fun: have a look online at different financial years around the world.

Update from Hayden:

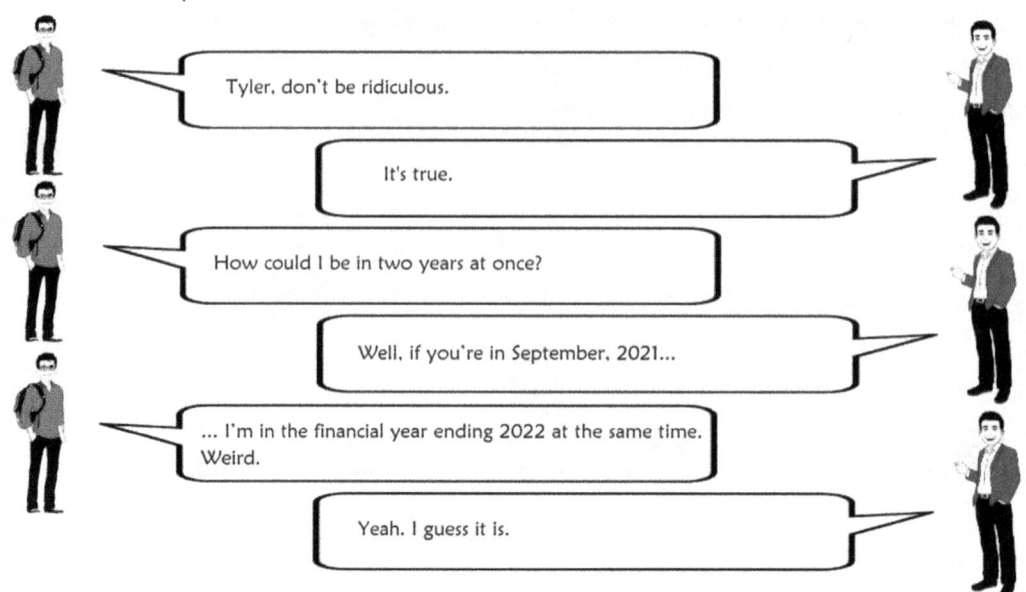

Hayden went to work one day and his boss gave him his PAYG summary for the 'end of the year'. In July. Hayden looked at him like he was crazy. But it makes sense. Hayden has a reminder in his phone to help him complete his tax return in August, so that he gets it submitted by the deadline in October.

Important Key Ideas!

Financial Year	The calendar for the business world: July 1 to June 30.
Calendar Year	The normal calendar: January 1 to December 31.
Tax Return Window	The four months to do your tax return! July 1 – Oct 31.
Tax Return Deadline	When your return is due - Halloween!

Mind the Gap

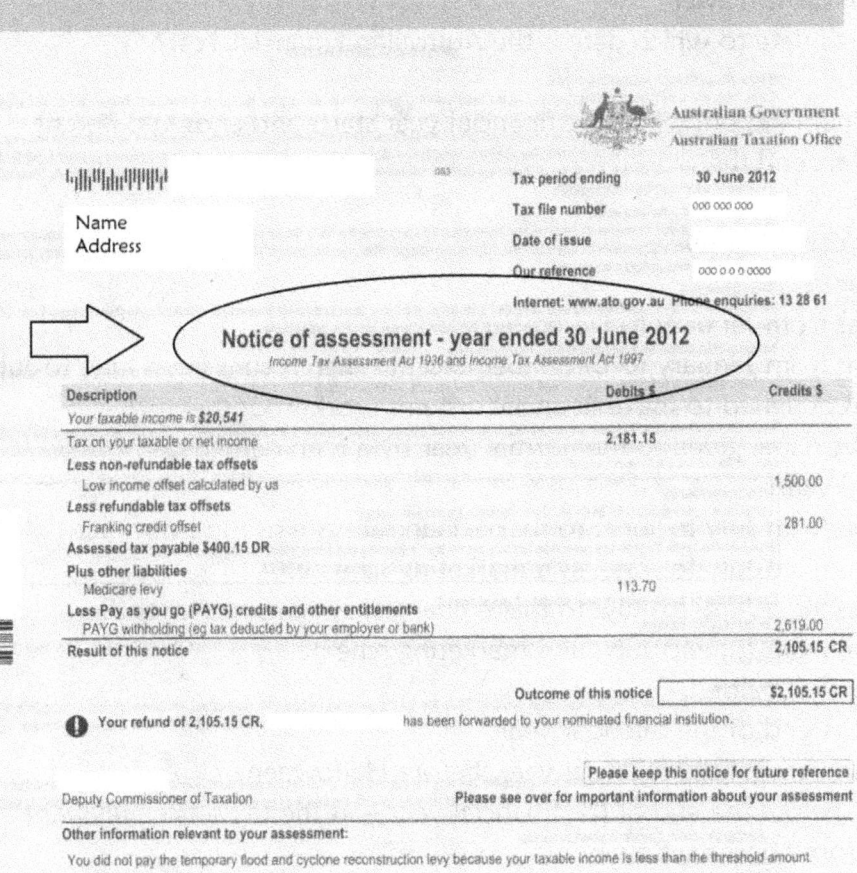

CHAPTER THREE QUIZ TIME!

1. From which date to which date is the Australian Financial Year?

2. Look online! Find out when the financial year starts and ends in different countries around the world!

Choose the most correct answer:

3. A calendar year:
    a. Runs from January to December.
    b. Runs from January to December except when it runs from June to July.
    c. Was designed to make financial systems work smoother.
    d. Is the name given to the normal year by a man named Cal.
4. A financial year:
    a. Runs from July to June, to make financial systems run smoother.
    b. Runs from July to June, as a marketing scheme.
    c. Runs from June to July, to make financial systems run smoother.
    d. Runs from June to July, as a marketing scheme.
5. All tax stuff is finalised:
    a. At the end of the calendar year.
    b. At the end of the financial year, before Halloween.
    c. Just before the end of the financial year – as the tax office will want information right away.
    d. More than a year after the year has ended – that's when all the information has been received.
6. It would be more difficult for the financial year to be the same as the calendar year because:
    a. Then there would be double the calculations to perform.
    b. The work would need to be done whilst everyone is away on the summer holidays.
    c. They already are the same.
    d. People would confuse their financial calculations with their calendar calculations.
7. The financial year:
    a. Is shared by the whole world.
    b. Is shared by all of Australia: people and corporations alike.
    c. Is shared by all of Australia, but sometimes a corporation is able to choose its own financial year.
    d. Is decided by each State in Australia.
8. "YE 16" means:
    a. Tax return number 16.

b. Financial year ending 2016 (Beginning 2015).
   c. Financial year ending 2016 (Beginning 2016, Jan 1st)
   d. Year Entry 2016, ending 2017.
9. The end of the financial year is busy because:
   a. Businesses are completing their records and doing paperwork.
   b. That's when all the best sales are. In fact the financial year was invented for this purpose.
   c. It's Christmas time and no one will be at work.
   d. Two years have passed by the end of each financial year.
10. The end of the financial year affects me because:
    a. Now I have Christmas in winter.
    b. My tax returns are due according to the financial year.
    c. It really doesn't affect me unless I have a business.
    d. Now there are two years in every year, which means I pay taxes twice.

Chapter Four: What is a TFN?

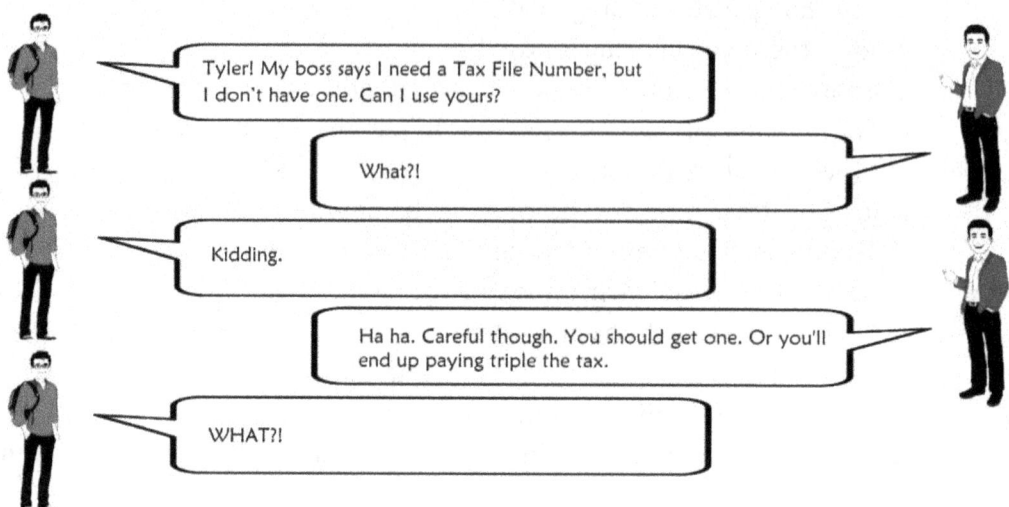

Why do I need to know this?
This chapter explains the *what*, *how* and *why* of tax file numbers.
1) Why do I need a tax file number?
2) How do I get a tax file number?
3) How do I use it?
4) How do I keep it safe?
5) How can a TFN save me money?
6) When should I get a TFN?
7) What happens if I don't get one?

What is a TFN?
A tax file number (TFN) is a personal identifier used by the ATO. It connects your tax documents to you, the person, and acts as a storage system.
In other words, it's your number. It's special to you, like your name.

Why do we need a tax file number?
Some years ago, the Australian government introduced a new filing system to simplify taxation. Every citizen was given a tax file number. Why? Let's say you're the Australian government. Can you imagine the amount of paperwork required to keep track of everyone in Australia? You'd need a system. So, you give every Australian a number: a tax file number, or TFN.

What do we use it for?
All our documentation is stored under our numbers:
1) When our boss pays our taxes out of our pay checks, it's recorded under that number.
2) Every time we fill out a tax document, we use that number.
3) Whenever the Tax Office needs our files, they look them up under that number.

That means that anyone who wants to work or earn money should have a TFN.

What's special about the number?
Names, addresses, contact information and jobs change all the time! But your tax file number stays the same always. Every tax file number is totally special and unique, and belongs entirely to that person. No one will ever have the same number as you, and no one needs two.

When should I get a TFN?
You can get a TFN at just about any time, but it's best to get one before you start your very first job. That could be at fourteen years old, seventeen years old, or twenty-one! Most people get them around 15-17, when they get a job and their first bosses tell them that they need one. If you're turning eighteen, you'll soon be a legal adult. You could get a TFN then, even if you're not working, because you might need it for other things and not just work.

What will happen if I don't get one?
Without a TFN, your boss is going to take almost half your pay check and give it to the tax office. Without a way of recording your earnings, the ATO isn't sure how much tax you have to pay, so they take as much as they can. If you don't have a TFN, you're taxed the highest possible rate! And you might miss out on other things as well. Because the TFN is so useful for identifying a person and all their records, it's used for more than just tax.

It's used for many important things:
1) Centrelink payments.
2) Superannuation accounts.
3) Certain debts (like university debts).
4) And more.

How can I stay safe with my TFN?
TFNs are very useful numbers for all Australians, but it can also be dangerous. A lot of people use other people's tax file numbers to steal their identities. That's why it's so important to keep it secret and safe at all times. Who do you think you should and shouldn't give the number to?
Friends?
Family?
Your boss?
Personal friends and even family members have no need for your TFN.
Your TFN isn't used for ordinary daily tasks, usually just larger tasks like getting a new job, or filing a tax return.
As a general rule, the only people who you should give your TFN to are the people who deal with your money.

That Includes:
- ✓ Your boss
- ✓ The tax office
- ✓ Centrelink
- ✓ Your superannuation provider
- ✓ Your bank

If you're not sure whether to give someone your TFN, ask them some questions:
1) Why do you need it?
2) What will you do with it?
3) What will happen if I don't provide it?

Then, to confirm it's the right thing to do, you can call the ATO to see if that person is allowed to ask for it.

How do you get a TFN?
The easiest way to apply for a TFN is...
1) To apply online through the ATO website, and then...
2) Book an appointment with your local post office to verify your identity.

Once you've had your interview at the post office, you'll be issued a TFN. There are instructions on the ATO website (**ato.gov.au**).

Your step-by-step guide to getting your TFN:

1) From the website, you can find 'get a tax file number' and 'apply online'. Fill out the form, which will ask you about your identity and will ask you to agree to a declaration. Print that out.
2) Go to the Australia post website. At **auspost.com.au,** you can book an appointment at your local post office.
3) Attend the appointment, and bring along your printed TFN application that you made in step one. Don't forget to bring some Identification.
4) Success!

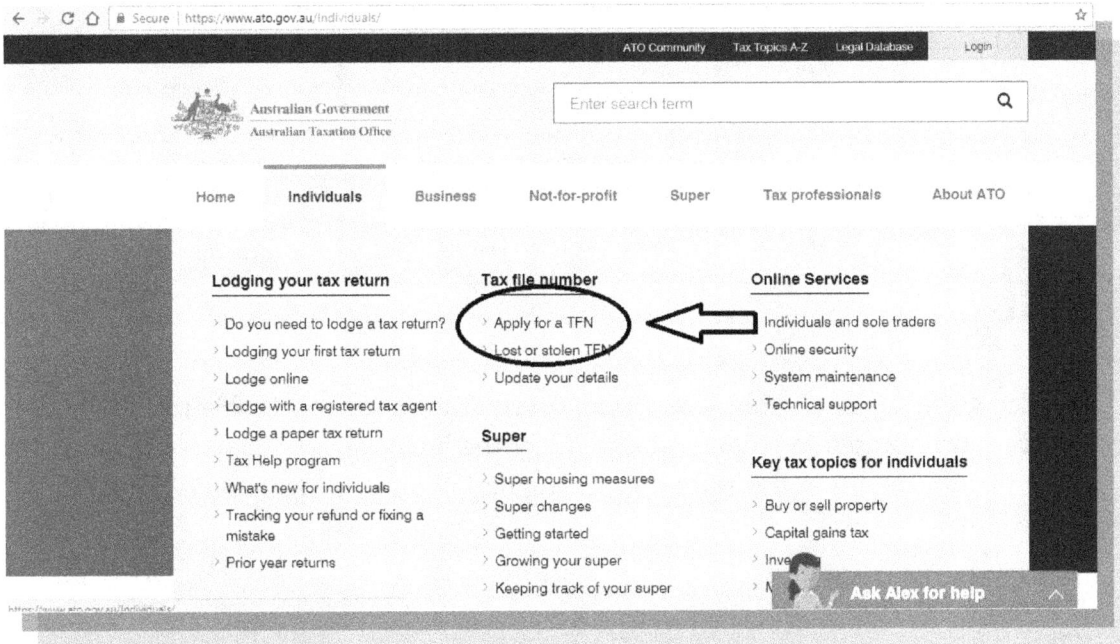

What kinds of ID should I bring?
You should bring along one primary form and two secondary forms of ID. Check the website for updated requirements.
Some primary forms include the following:
- Your Aussie birth certificate.
- Your passport.
- Your citizenship certificate if you were born overseas.

Secondary forms of ID can include the following:
- A Medicare card.
- A bank account statement.
- A student card.

If you are under 16, you may only need one form of secondary identification.

Tips and Tricks!
1) Get your TFN sooner rather than later: so you won't pay too much tax!
2) Contact the ATO if you're confused about the TFN process.
3) Don't share your TFN unless you have a good reason.
4) Keep your TFN number letter (they'll print a letter and send it to you!) with your other tax documents in a safe place.

Update from Hayden:

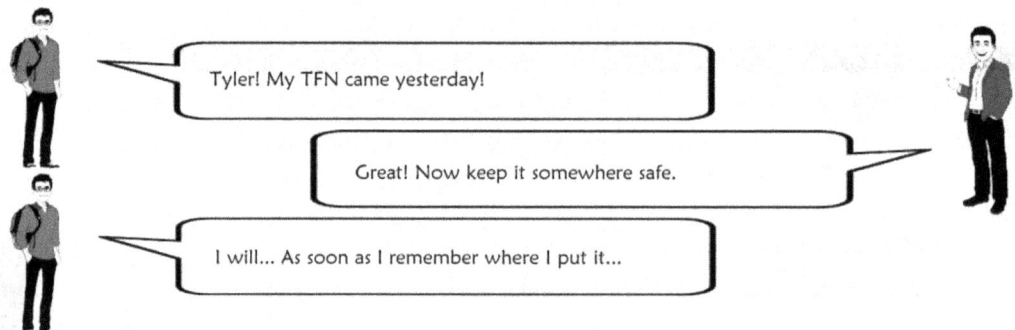

Tyler! My TFN came yesterday!

Great! Now keep it somewhere safe.

I will... As soon as I remember where I put it...

Hayden got his TFN and his wages were taxed at the proper rate. He put his letter in a folder and stored it in a filing cabinet. Over the financial year, Hayden put his other tax documents in this folder, including his tax assessments and PAYG summaries.

Important Key Ideas!

TFN	Tax file number.
Primary ID	Important ID, like your passport and driver's licence.
Secondary ID	Slightly less important ID, like your Medicare card and bank statements.
Tax rate	The percentage of your money that the government takes.
ATO Website	www.ato.gov.au
Australia Post Website	www.auspost.com.au

Here's a copy of an old TFN Advice:
(the letter they send you when you get your TFN)

TAX FILE NUMBER ADVICE

In reply to your recent application/enquiry, your tax file number (TFN) is:

000 000 000

Keep this notice in a safe place for further reference.

Please note that you only need one TFN. Your TFN will stay the same regardless of your changing circumstances. For example, you do not need a new TFN if you move interstate, change jobs, change your name in any way, have investments, or claim government benefits.

You are not required to disclose your TFN to any person and the misuse of TFNs can result in penalties. However, you should quote your TFN in all future dealings with us and, if you receive any benefits or entitlements from Centrelink/Family Assistance Office (FAO), you must advise them immediately of the above TFN.

Other organisations to which a TFN may be quoted can include:
- your employer or payer
- investment bodies such as banks, building societies and credit unions with which you hold funds on deposit
- superannuation funds, and
- educational institutions.

For more information on TFNs phone 13 28 61 between 8am and 6pm Monday to Friday or visit www.ato.gov.au.

Yours sincerely

CHAPTER FOUR QUIZ TIME!

Which of the following would you give your TFN to? Write "yes" or "no".
1) Your boss.
2) Your brother's best friend Steve.
3) Your superannuation provider.
4) The guy you're buying a bike from.
5) Your facebook page.
6) Your business cards.
7) The ATO.
8) Your accountant.
9) Your application for a higher-education debt.
10) Your guitar teacher.

11. A tax file number is:
    a. The file at the tax office which holds the tax information for my family.
    b. A personal identifier – a number that identifies me to the Tax Office.
    c. The number allocated to each tax return as it is submitted (different for each tax return).
    d. The amount of accrued taxes filed over the year.
    e. All of the above
12. Why do we need a tax file number at all?
    a. Because the government can't legally refer to people by their names.
    b. Because names and other personal information can be changed, and the number cannot.
    c. To stop workplace bullying.
    d. For us to use when we buy new tax files from a stationary store.
13. I get a new tax file number:
    a. When I change my name.
    b. Every time I get a new job.
    c. Only once in my life.
    d. When I change bank accounts.
14. A good time to get your tax file number is when:
    a. You get your first job or before – you CANNOT work without a tax file number.
    b. You get your first job or before – as soon as you can.
    c. One floats down from the sky, because life is that easy.
    d. As late as you can, so you don't have to pay taxes for ages.
15. My tax file number is dangerous because:
    a. If I lose it, the government can fine me.
    b. It makes me pay taxes.

        c. Someone can use it for identity theft.

        d. If I use it wrong, I lose a lot of money in taxes.
16. The government uses the TFN system primarily to:

        a. Keep track of how much money people spend.

        b. Make us pay as much tax as possible.

        c. Help the government interact with other world governments.

        d. Stay organised in tax.
17. I am required by law to provide my tax file number to:

        a. Anyone that asks for it.

        b. Customs, on the way into Australia, to prove I am Australian.

        c. My extended family.

        d. None of the above.
18. A tax file number can be used for things other than tax, including:

        a. Keeping track of the government.

        b. Getting in and out of Australia, like a passport.

        c. Obtaining Centrelink support.

        d. Make purchases instead of using a bank account and card.

        e. All of the above.
19. A good way to apply for a tax file number is to:

        a. Present your birth certificate to your tax agent and ask him to get you one.

        b. You don't need to get one – your parents have always had one for you.

        c. You don't need to apply – the government will send you one.

        d. Apply online and go to the post office.
20. When your new boss gives you a form asking for your tax file number, called a TFN declaration form, you should:

        a. Call the police, he is trying to steal money from you.

        b. Fill out the form, and give copies to everyone in your new workplace.

        c. Fill out the form, and send it to your accountant.

        d. Fill out the form and return it to your boss.

Chapter Five:
What are the Main Tax Documents?

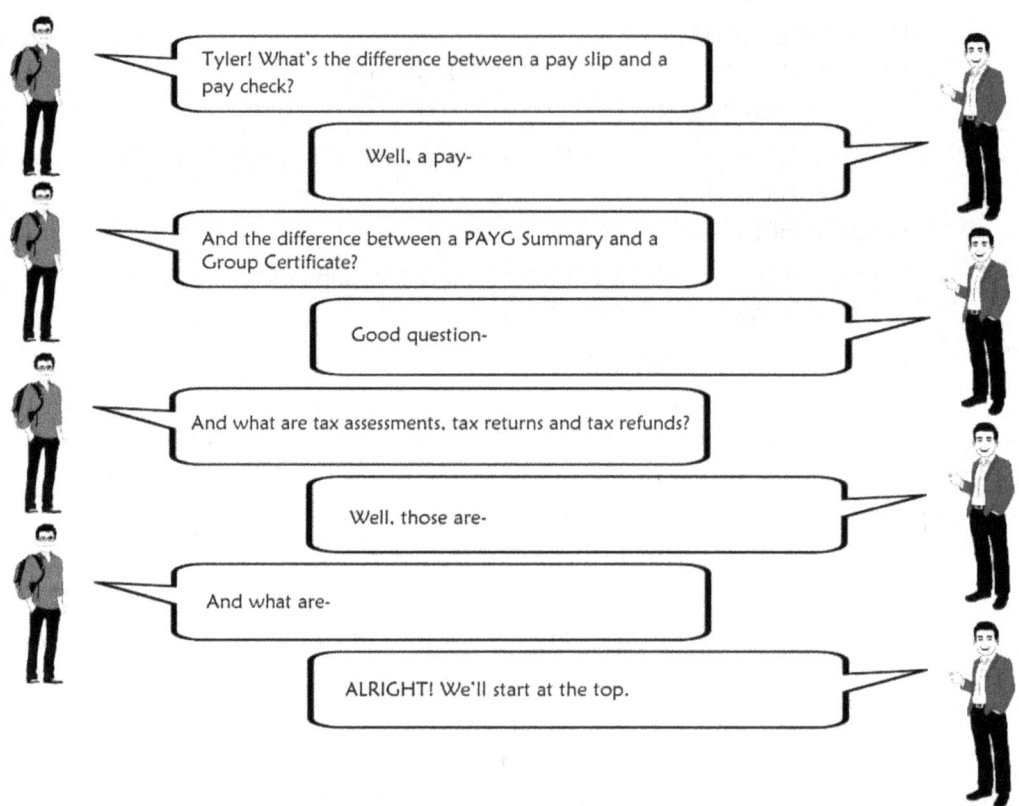

Why do I need this chapter?

This chapter explains the sequence of tax documents, and the *how* of the income tax process.
1) What documents do I have to understand, use, and store?
2) How does everything fit together in the big picture? Why are things done this way?
3) What do I have to do, and when?

What are the Tax Documents?

Tax documents are prepared in a certain order and system. First, you will receive a **PAYG summary**, which you use to complete a **tax return**, and that in turn is needed by the ATO to make your **tax assessment**.

How many and which documents do I have to know?
There are five important ones for now:
1) TFN Declaration Form (you fill this out only once per job!)
2) Pay slip
3) PAYG Summary
4) Tax Return
5) Tax Assessment

What are the documents, and how do they work?
Your TFN Declaration Form:
This is an official form that you use to write down your TFN and some other information about yourself and your employment. It's needed for your boss to know how much to pay you, and how much to take out in tax and in repayments of university debts, for example.

Your Pay slip:
This is an easier one. This is what you get when you're paid. It shows you how much you were paid, how much tax you paid, and how many hours you worked. You won't need this to file a tax return. It's just for you, to make sure you understand how you're paid, and for you to check that your boss has calculated your wages properly. To clarify, your pay check is the **money** you get, and your pay slip is the **paper** that explains your wages.

Your PAYG Payment Summary:
This is also called a group certificate (there's no real difference!). This is your summary of your wages and taxes for the year. Your boss prepares this and sends it to you, so that you have all the information you need to complete your tax return.

Your Tax Return:
This is your declaration of all your earnings and all relevant information from the past year. You include how much you earned from all incomes (maybe you have more than one job, or investments), and send it to them so that they can prepare your tax assessment. Your **tax return** is a **document** you complete, and a **tax refund** is the **money** you get back if you've paid too much in tax.

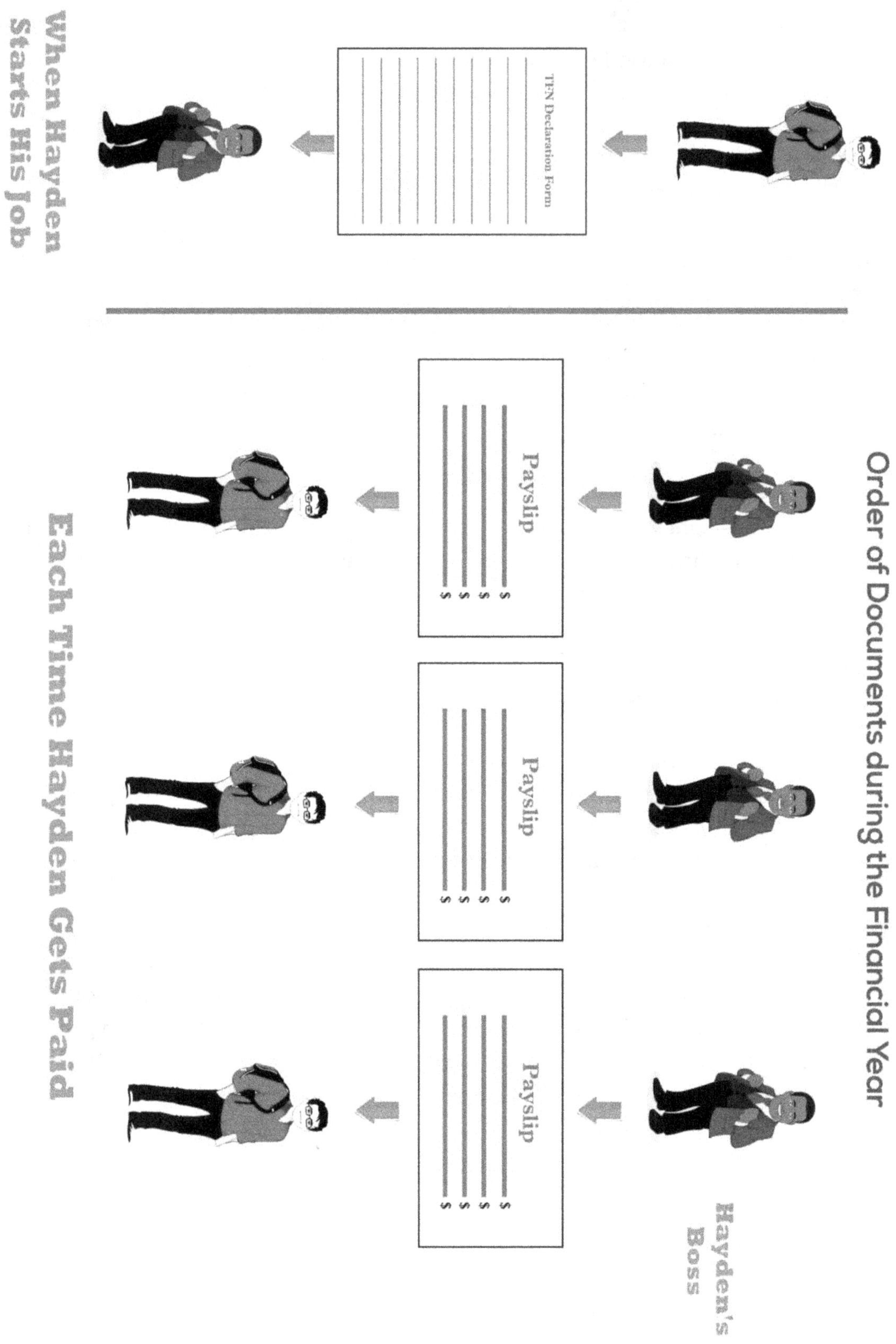

Mind the Gap

Order of Documents during the Financial Year

When Hayden Starts His Job

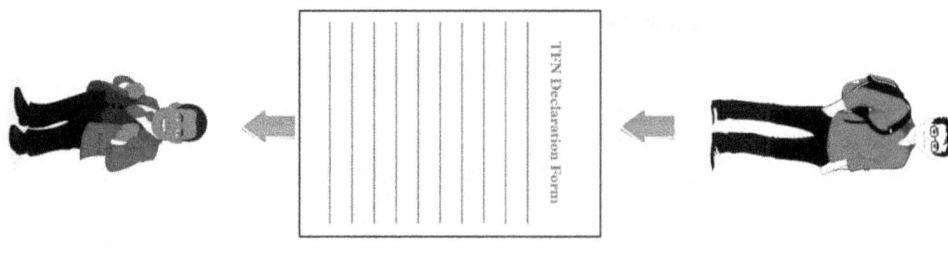

Hayden's Boss → TFN Declaration Form → Hayden

Each Time Hayden Gets Paid

Hayden's Boss → Payslip → Hayden

Hayden's Boss → Payslip → Hayden

Hayden's Boss → Payslip → Hayden

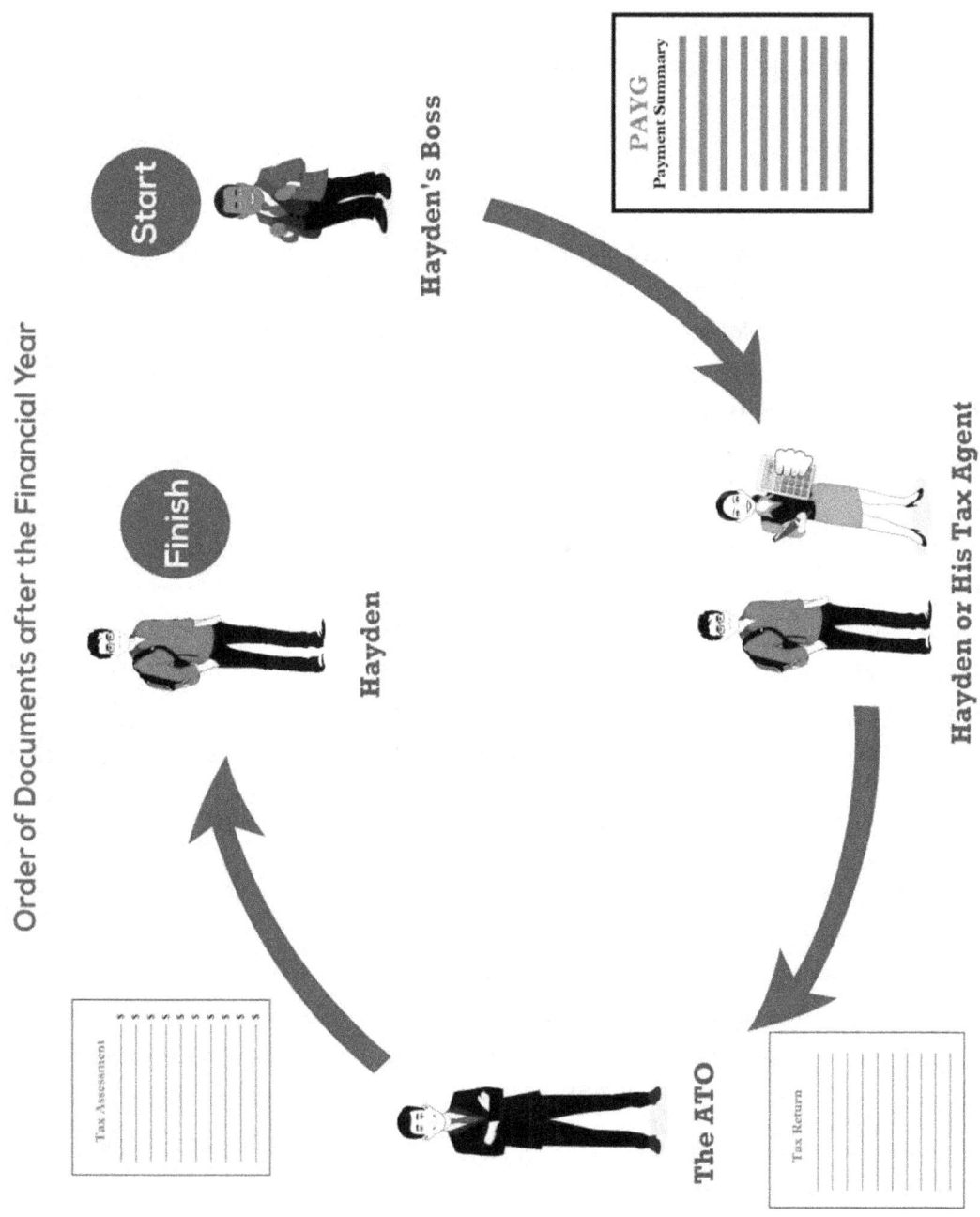

Your Notice of Assessment:
(Also called your tax assessment)
Once the ATO has all your information, they will check through everything you've said and do some calculations to find out how much tax you were supposed to pay. Once they find that out, they then look at how much you actually paid. If you didn't pay enough, you will have to pay more. If you paid too much, they'll give you some back. They write down that information in a tax assessment and send it to you.

All of this is done in this way because it's the most efficient method that the ATO could think of. After all, there is a lot of information to collect. **See the next couple of chapters for more information on each of these documents!**

So... What do I have to do?
Your biggest task is to complete your tax return between the 1st of July and the 31st of October. You can (and maybe should) get a tax accountant to help you with your tax return, and also check out the tax return chapter of this book. The other stuff is mostly taken care of for you (your PAYG summary is sent to you, and so is your tax assessment).

Tips and Tricks!
How can you avoid costly mistakes?
1) Keep track of your documents carefully – don't throw away your PAYG summary just because you don't know what it is!
2) Get help preparing your tax return, and do it on time! You might get some money back and avoid a fee.
3) Provide the right information! Lies and missed opportunities are costly (see other chapters and your tax accountant).
4) If you don't understand, ask for help or check a reputable website or the correct chapter of this book. Knowledge is power!
5) Read up on each step carefully in the appropriate chapter of this book so that you can work quickly and accurately! See the *tax deductions* and *tax returns* sections.

Update from Hayden!

Understanding the bigger picture helped Hayden: he knew when and why certain things had to be done. He was able to make a stronger plan and when he received a letter in the mail, he understood what it was and what to do with it.

Important Key Ideas!

Pay Slip	A paper from your boss that explains your pay.
Pay cheque	The money you receive for your work.
PAYG Summary	The summary of your wages for the year.
Group Certificate	The same thing as your PAYG Summary.
Tax Return	A document you provide to the ATO with your income and personal information.
Tax Refund	The money you get back if you paid too much in taxes.
Tax Assessment	The letter from the ATO explaining how much tax you owe/get back.

CHAPTER FIVE QUIZ TIME!
Number these documents in the order you receive them (A,B,C, and D):
1. PAYG Summary   ___
2. Tax Assessment   ___
3. Tax Return   ___
4. Pay Slip   ___

True or False:
5. Pay slips are generally used to fill in tax returns.
6. PAYG summaries are used to fill in tax returns.
7. Tax assessments are used to fill in tax returns.
8. Pay slips are given to you by the government.
9. Tax assessments are given to you by the government (ATO).
10. Tax returns contain information about how much you earned.
11. You won't be able to file a tax return until you get your tax assessment.
12. You don't get a tax assessment until after you complete your tax return.
13. PAYG summaries contain a summary of what you earned that year.
14. The only important document is your tax return.

Multiple Choice:
15. A tax return is (careful!):
    a. When you "return" money to the government, because you didn't pay enough taxes.
    b. When the government returns money to you for paying too much tax during the year.
    c. A form you fill out to help the tax office do a final tax count for the year just passed.
    d. When the form you filled out about the year just passed is returned to you.
16. A tax assessment is:
    a. The results you get back from the tax office, after you've submitted your tax return.
    b. When the government thinks about changing tax law.
    c. Something most people rarely have to deal with.
    d. A formal university exam for accountants.
17. A tax refund is:
    a. The money the government returns to you for over-paid taxes during the financial year.
    b. When the government wrongfully taxes you due to an error, and they give the money back.

       c. When you pay the extra bit of tax you haven't yet paid during the year.
       d. When your tax return is reviewed years later, and a mistake is discovered.
18. A pay slip is:
       a. Something you usually use when you complete a tax return.
       b. Something that tells you how much you earned in your pay period.
       c. Something that is often used to prove that the ATO has made a mistake.
       d. All of the above.
19. Tax assessments, tax returns, and PAYG payment summaries are processed every:
       a. Five years.
       b. Year.
       c. Month.
       d. Week.
       e. Pay cheque.

Chapter Six:
What is Tax Withholding?

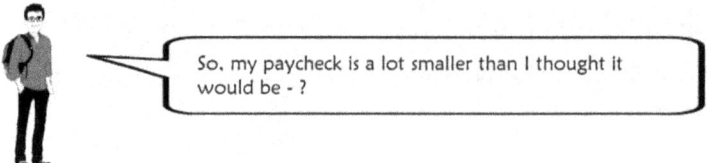

Why do I need this chapter?
This chapter explains the *how* and *when* of paying taxes.
1) How and when do I actually pay my taxes?
2) How is my withholding rate calculated?
3) How can I make sure I'm being charged the right rate?

> **What is Withholding?**
> "Withholding" is the way we pay income tax (pay-as-you-go).
> They are the taxes that are taken from your pay check every time you get paid.

Yes, you read correctly.
1) Income tax
2) Withholding tax
3) PAYG tax

They're all different ways to explain the same thing.

How and when is income tax paid?
How can we pay?
Do we walk into a tax office every week and pay with cash or credit?
Do we send it off online somewhere or post a cheque?
In reality, as an employee, it's all done automatically for you. Your boss takes it out of your pay check and sends it to the ATO for you. Once, it's set up, you don't have to think about it! It happens every time you're paid, whether that's weekly, fortnightly or monthly.

Why is it paid automatically?
Why can't I be in control of when and how and where I pay my income tax?
Can you imagine asking everyone to line up and pay their taxes at their local ATO

or government office on a Friday afternoon? Nobody would do it! Then the government would have to chase them for the money.

Instead, your boss withholds your taxes. That means he takes them out and holds them in his own bank account before sending them off to the ATO for you. He then sends you your pay cheque. It's easier for you and safer for the government: they can be certain they're getting their money, because legally, your boss must take them out before he gives you your hard-earned pay cheque.

How much are they going to take out?

Good question. Unfortunately, the answer is not very simple.

The government knows that over the course of any given year people change jobs, their incomes go up or down, things just change. Because the government doesn't know for sure how much you're going to earn in the year, they don't know how much tax you have to pay until the whole year is over.

But they're not going to wait until the end of the year for you to pay your tax. They need the money to keep the country running! So they make some assumptions about you and your income and they basically **choose an amount that seems right to them**, and they take that amount from your pay check. They have a system for calculating how much tax to take out, but it's still only an estimate of what your taxes will end up being at the end of the year.

What if they take too much withholding tax?

They usually do. But don't worry, you get it back later. The government takes out what ever seems right, and at the end of the year they do all the maths properly and see how much tax you are really supposed to have paid for the year. If you've paid too much, you get the extra bit back. It's called a tax refund.

And what if they don't take enough?

The ATO will send you a bill at the end of the financial year.

Most of the time, regular employees get tax refunds at the end of the year. But not always. Especially if you haven't been telling the ATO the truth about something, or maybe you didn't fill something out correctly. Then they might ask you for the rest of the money at the end of the year.

How do they work out your taxes at the end of the year?

The answer: your tax return. A tax return is your summary of everything important for the year, including everything you've earned, and from there the ATO figures out who owes who what.

Then they usually send you a letter telling you what they've discovered. That letter is called your tax assessment. It's a final summary of your taxes for the year, and it tells you how much you'll get back, or what you owe.

How do they work out how much tax to take out?
First, the ATO makes a set of rules about how much should be taken out.
(the rules depend on how much your earn, and some other stuff)
These rules come in the form of...
1) a special online calculator on the ATO website, OR...
2) a giant table of numbers, also on the ATO website.

For example, if you earned $2305.80 this week (that would be a very high income indeed), you can find $2306 (the closest listed number) in the income table, and next to it, the ATO has listed how much tax should be taken out.

Check the table.
How much is the withholding (with the tax-free threshold)?

It's $662.00.

Crazy table, right?
Too many numbers...
But it's easy enough to use once you know how.

Weekly tax table

Weekly earnings 1 $	Amount to be withheld		Weekly earnings 1 $	Amount to be withheld	
	With tax-free threshold 2 $	No tax-free threshold 3 $		With tax-free threshold 2 $	No tax-free threshold 3 $
2301.00	661.00	797.00	2386.00	694.00	830.00
2302.00	661.00	797.00	2387.00	694.00	830.00
2303.00	661.00	797.00	2388.00	694.00	831.00
2304.00	662.00	798.00	2389.00	695.00	831.00
2305.00	662.00	798.00	2390.00	695.00	831.00
2306.00	662.00	799.00	2391.00	696.00	832.00
2307.00	663.00	799.00	2392.00	696.00	832.00
2308.00	663.00	799.00	2393.00	696.00	833.00
2309.00	664.00	800.00	2394.00	697.00	833.00
2310.00	664.00	800.00	2395.00	697.00	833.00
2311.00	664.00	801.00	2396.00	698.00	834.00
2312.00	665.00	801.00	2397.00	698.00	834.00
2313.00	665.00	801.00	2398.00	698.00	834.00
2314.00	666.00	802.00	2399.00	699.00	835.00
2315.00	666.00	802.00	2400.00	699.00	835.00

Careful! This tax table might be out of date.

Sometimes your boss gets it wrong. Everyone's human.
But that's why you should check up on him/her.

How can I make sure I'm being charged the right rate?
So guess what? That table and calculator can be used by you too!
Look up your rates yourself. If it doesn't seem right, ask your boss about it!
If you're still not convinced, write down what your boss said about it, and then ask the ATO if it's correct.

... If the ATO agrees it's not right, then it's time to take things further to get what you're entitled to. The ATO can advise you, and you can also go to the Fair Work Ombudsmen (a government agency that protects employees, look them up!).

Tips and Tricks!
1) Look up your withholding rates on the ATO website!
2) Check your pay slips carefully to make sure you were paid the correct amount for the number of hours that you worked. In fact, check that all details are correct!
3) Keep your payslips in case there is a problem later.

Update from Hayden!

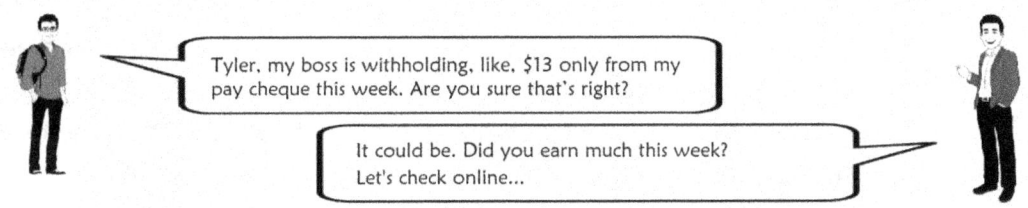

Hayden was careful to check his payslips. He checked how many hours he worked, how much he was paid per hour, and his total pay. He also checked that his boss was withholding the correct amount of taxes. Pretty good for someone who never liked this kind of stuff.

Important Key Ideas!

Tax Withholding and Pay-As-You-Go	These are both terms to describe the way we pay **income tax**, which is a tax on what we earn.
Tax Rate	The percentages (or bands) of tax that a person pays on their income.
Withholding Rate	The amount of money withheld from a pay check to pay for income tax.
ATO Withholding Calculator	A program online from the ATO that calculates how much should be withheld from a person's pay.

CHAPTER SIX QUIZ TIME!

1. An employee's income taxes are paid:
    a. By cash or card at any ATO shop front.
    b. By deducting directly from a person's pay.
    c. In the same way electricity or water bills are paid – a bill is sent in the post.
    d. Whichever way you choose to pay.
2. Withholding is when:
    a. You ask the government to take the tax out before you earn your wages.
    b. When your taxes are held with your wages in the same place for a long time.
    c. The period of time between when your boss pays you, and when you pay your taxes on that income.
    d. When your boss takes your taxes out of your pay and gives it to the tax office.
3. As an employee, who takes your taxes from your wages and sends it to the government?
    a. Your boss.
    b. The government.
    c. You.
    d. Your parents.
4. Under the PAYG system, you pay your taxes to the ATO:
    a. Every time you're paid.
    b. Every week.
    c. Every month.
    d. Whenever you "pass go", as they say in monopoly.
5. Income tax and PAYG tax are...
    a. Different. One taxes you on your income, and the other taxes you on what you pay out in living expenses.
    b. Pretty much the same thing. PAYG is the *frequency of payment* for income taxes. It just means you pay your income tax "as you go".
    c. Different. You only pay one of the two – you get to choose.
    d. Different. You only pay one of the two – it depends on your job.
6. Your taxes are taken out:
    a. Before you begin work, based on estimates of what you will earn.
    b. After the work is done, but before you are paid.
    c. After you are paid the full amount, you then pay the taxes yourself.
    d. It's up to you.

7. The amount of tax withheld is:
    a. Decided according to the tax office's rates and set of rules.
    b. Decided by your boss, depending on how long he thinks you will work for him.
    c. Are usually double what the tax office thinks you need to pay, just to be safe.
    d. Decided by you.
    e. None of the above.
8. If you pay too much in withholding:
    a. You'll never get it back, so make sure to barter the rate down with your boss.
    b. You'll have to file a complaint with the ATO to get your money back.
    c. You can't pay too much in withholding. The ATO is too careful and takes exactly the correct amount each time.
    d. It'll be returned to you at the end of the financial year.

Chapter Seven:
What is a Tax File Number Declaration Form? And How Do I Fill One Out?

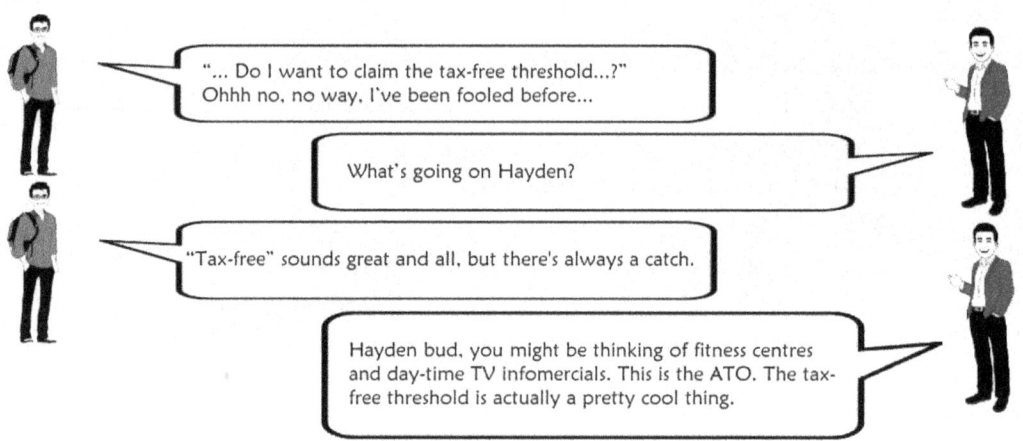

Why do I need this chapter?
This chapter explores the *how* of filling out a TFN declaration for a new job.
1) What do these questions really mean?
2) What happens if I answer incorrectly?
3) Help me get through this faster!
4) What is the tax free threshold, and how can I use it to reduce my tax withholding?

What is a TFN Declaration Form?
A TFN Declaration Form is a form that an employee fills out and gives to his/her employer so that their wages are paid and taxed properly. It gives employers necessary information about TFNs, relevant debts, and the employee's situation.

What is this form and why do I need it?

In short, you need it so you're paid and taxed properly.

Any and all bosses provide new employees with one to fill out.

The information it gives them includes...
1) Your personal info (name, address).
2) Your TFN (to direct your taxes to the ATO under your name).
3) Your status about particular tax offsets you could claim.
4) Your status about certain debts, like university debts.

> This section gives general advice only about TFN declaration forms. It does not take into account your personal circumstances. If you are not certain about the answer you should provide, seek help from the ATO or a tax expert. Your boss and parents might be good help too.

How do I answer Question Two?

Do you authorise your payer to give your TFN to the trustee of your superannuation fund?

Many people answer yes. These facts are true:
- Superannuation is money your boss puts into a bank account for you, for when you are old.
- Your boss legally must pay you superannuation.
- After you fill out this form, your boss will have your TFN (he needs it!).
- Your superannuation account needs your TFN, too.
- If you tick this box, your boss will give your superannuation provider your TFN.
- If you don't tick this box, your super fund will contact you to get your TFN, anyway.

By ticking this box, you save time because your boss can do that step for you.

Note: see other *Mind the Gap* works about what superannuation is and what your options are.

How do I answer Question Six?

On what basis are you paid?

People are employed with different expectations:
- Some are employed full-time (38ish hours a week).
- Some are employed part-time (fewer than 38ish hours per week).
- Some are employed casually (sometimes many hours, sometimes few hours per week).

- Labour hire is more complicated, and less common. It's when one company sends you to different workplaces for different work.
- Superannuation – this is when you are receiving your superannuation benefits, when you retire.

In essence, this form is asking you what type of employment you have. This information will help the ATO decide how much tax to withhold.

If you don't know the answer, you should ask your boss which form of employment you have with him.

For more information on employment stuff (minimum wages, benefits, super, unions and more), see *Mind the Gap: Your Job*!

How do I answer Question Seven?
Are you an Australian resident for tax purposes?
Most people would say yes. If you live in Australia most of the time, you are most-likely a resident for tax purposes.

Who isn't a resident for tax purposes, then?
If someone comes to Australia to work for a short period of time (a few weeks or months, for example), they may not be a resident for tax purposes.
If you aren't permanently living in Australia (at least for this financial year), or you're not sure, you'll have to call the ATO, or go to the ATO website (where you can take a little test to see if you're a resident or not).
But otherwise, tick yes.

How do I answer Question Eight?
This is the harder one.
Do you wish to claim the tax-free threshold?
1) If you have only one job, tick yes.
2) If you have more than one job, tick yes for one job (the one you work the most), and no for the others.

What does this question mean?
In short, everyone gets to earn some money every year without paying tax.
That's the tax-free threshold. Currently, at the time of printing this book, it's $18,200 a year. So if you don't earn more than that in a year, you'll pay no tax. If you earn a little more, you'll pay a small rate of tax. If you earn a lot, you'll pay a much higher rate!
The more you earn, the more you pay, but also the higher rate you pay:

First, 0%...
Then 19% for the next amount of money you earn...
Then 32.5% for the next lot of money, etc...

So if you don't earn much, your boss won't take much tax out because he (and the ATO) knows you probably won't earn more than the tax-free threshold.
(Be careful! The tax bands are often different if you're in Australia on a visa, ie, you're not Australian and you're travelling here!)

So why don't I get the tax free threshold on all my jobs then? What difference does it make where I earn the money, if it's one job or three? Why am I taxed so much more? That's pretty unfair...

Hold up. On the surface it might seem unfair, but that's not the case at all.
In the end, you'll pay **exactly the same amount of tax.**

Imagine this situation:
Sarah likes to work in different places. She has four jobs! She works one day in each job. When she filled out her four TFN Declaration Forms (one for each time she got a new job), she claimed the tax-free threshold each time!
This is not a good thing.
Her bosses don't know how many jobs she has. All they know is that...
   1) She claimed the tax-free threshold, and
   2) She wasn't earning much money at their workplace.
So, they each took almost 0% tax, because it was predicted she wouldn't earn more than the $18,000 threshold (because they didn't know she was working multiple jobs: they don't keep records of ALL of her employment).
In reality, because she had four jobs, she was earning a lot of money.

So anyway, at the end of the financial year, the ATO realised she had actually earned a lot of money, but her bosses never took the tax out. Suddenly, she owed a lot of money. She got a big tax bill in the mail. She was shocked, to say the least, and it took her some time to pay it off.

How much tax do people pay?
Your question is about the tax bands. You can see them online!
In Australia, the more you earn, the higher percentage of tax you pay. Bosses look at your pay cheque and take out a lot of or a little tax depending on how much you earn. You can imagine that if you had several jobs, none of your bosses REALLY

know how much you earned. So they might not tax enough tax.

For more specific information on the tax bands, check the end of this book. Also, you can check the ATO website!

How do I answer Question Nine?
Do you want to claim the seniors and pensioners tax offset?
This one is easier. Are you a senior (65 years old or older) or a pensioner (an old person with a small income from the government)? Probably not.
Then tick no!
A tax offset is when certain people get a tax discount. Old people might get one because they don't have much money. But you can't get this one because you're not old! Are you?

How do I answer Question Ten?
Do you want to claim a zone, overseas forces or invalid carer offset?
This one is also a bit easier.
Are you in the army? No?
Do you care for (pay for and take care of, like a parent) a disabled person? No?
Chances are, the answer is no for you for this question. If there's a possibility the answer might be yes, check with a tax professional or the ATO. But most people **should tick no.**

"Zone and overseas forces" means army here.
"Invalid" means disabled person here.
"Offset" means tax discount.

How do I answer Question Eleven?
Do you have a Higher Education Loan Program (HELP) or Trade Support Loan (TSL) debt?
A HELP debt is special loan from the government to help people pay for their education costs.
A TSL debt is similar, for trade studies.
Have you been to university? Have you taken out one of these special debts from the government?
If the answer is yes, tick yes.
If you're under 17, the answer is probably no.
A financial supplement debt is another loan that's similar. It helps with other costs while studying.
Have you taken one of these loans? **If not, tick no.**

What happens if I answer these questions incorrectly?
You could end up with a tax bill at the end of the year, or possibly they'll take way too much tax from your pay cheque and you'll receive a smaller take-home pay. In the end it should work out fairly, but it could take the whole financial year to straighten it out. Imagine waiting a full year for your money! What a waste. You could have invested it and got MORE money in that time.

In some situations, you could end up with legal issues. Best be careful!

Example TFN Declaration Form:

Tips and Tricks!
1) Be careful with the tax-free threshold and the HELP debt questions – these could have financial ramifications.
2) If you're unsure, you have many places to go to from help: the ATO and your boss for starters.
3) The more questions you ask of knowledgeable people, the better off you will be.

Update from Hayden!

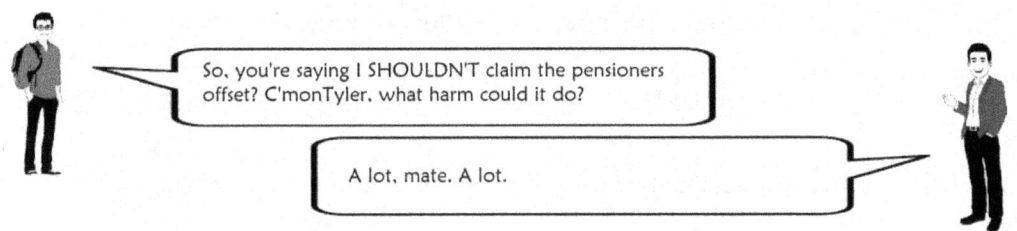

The more TFN forms Hayden fills out over his lifetime, the easier they'll get.

Important Key Ideas!

Tax offset	A tax discount.
HELP and TSL Debts	University and studies debts.
Superannuation	Savings (from your boss) for when you're older.
Full-time	Working 38ish hours per week.
Part-time	Working fewer than 38ish hours per week.
Casual	Working different hours every week.
Australian resident for tax purposes	Someone who lives in Australia and pays tax like an Australian.

CHAPTER SEVEN QUIZ TIME!
Yes or no questions:

1) Is it a good idea to claim the tax-free threshold for each of my several jobs?

2) Is it a good idea to claim the tax-free threshold if I earn a lot of money, even if I only have one job?

3) Is the tax-free threshold available to
    a. certain workers in certain industries only, or
    b. just about every Australian regardless of industry?

4) Is the tax-free threshold only available to part-time and casual workers?

5) Is it a good idea to claim the tax-free threshold if I might change my one job to a different one job?

6) Would most Australian teenagers claim the invalid tax offset?

7) Are Australian people who fill out tax returns and work in Australia in the long term residents for tax purposes?

8) Is it true that I shouldn't let my boss provide my TFN to my superannuation provider, because it's unsafe?

9) Is the zone and overseas forces offset for soldiers and people in the army?

10) Is a tax offset a good thing if you want to save money?

Chapter Eight:
What is a PAYG Payment Summary?

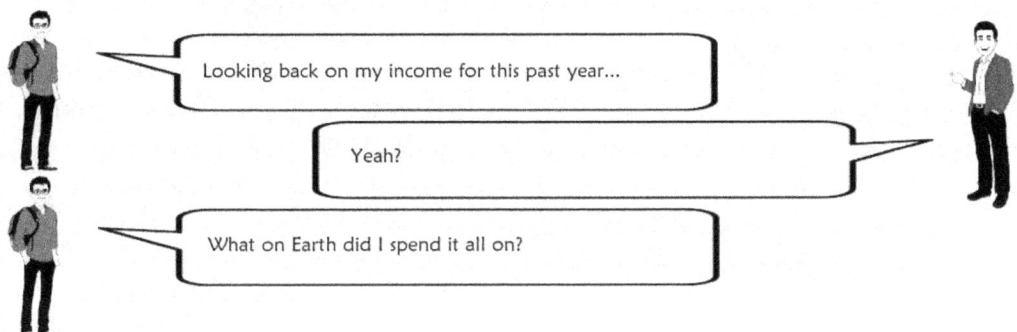

Why do I need this chapter?
This chapter explores the *what* and *why* of PAYG Payment Summaries.
1) What are they?
2) Why do I need them?
3) What do I do with them?
4) How do I read a PAYG summary? What do the numbers really mean?
5) What does it mean for me and my job? How can I use it to make decisions about my career?
6) What happens if I use it incorrectly or lose it?
7) What's a group certificate?
8) What's the difference between a PAYG payment summary and a pay slip?

What is a PAYG Payment Summary?
A PAYG Payment Summary (also known as a group certificate) is a document from your boss that summarises what you've earned in one financial year, how much tax you've paid, and related information.

Where did this thing come from?
Your boss sends your PAYG Summary to you at the end of the financial year. Legally, he has to, because you need that information to complete a tax return. Most people don't keep such good records of their own incomes each and every week (that would be a lot of careful work!), but your boss has to.
He sends you a copy.
If you have more than one boss, they will each send you a summary. You'll have

one for each job. You might even get other documents from other companies, like your health insurance provider, for example. Your health insurance policy can also affect your tax for high income earners, so they might send you some information to help you lodge your return.

When does it come?
After the financial year has ended: July 1.

What's really happening here is that tax returns can be prepared after July 1, so companies (anyone that gives you an income or affects your tax situation) send you the information you need to complete it.

What's on the PAYG Payment Summary?
What does this information mean?
It includes a lot of information:
- A total of how much you've been paid for the whole year for that job.
- How much tax has been taken out (withheld) for the whole year for that job.
- Any allowances or extra benefits your job gave you (like if they gave you money to stay in a hotel). Some of these are tax free, some are not!
- Any deductions from your pay. You might, for example, decide to put extra money into your superannuation. That can sometimes be deducted directly from your pay.
- Other details like your TFN and the dates of the summary.

How do I use it for my tax return?
And how can it help me learn more about my job?
The purpose for the PAYG Payment Summary is to help you file a tax return. Doing your taxes might be a bit boring. If you give your summary to a tax accountant, he can do it for you, and possibly save you money, too.

Beyond that practical use, it's also a great document to help you learn about your job. Here, you can see exactly how much you earn in a year, and what other forms of income you got from your job (allowances, benefits). This is the best way to get a clear monetary understanding of your job, to compare it with other jobs out there.

Also, you can see how much tax your boss is withholding. You can see your before-tax and after-tax income, and any other relevant information.

What's a Group Certificate?
Some bosses don't call these documents PAYG Payment Summaries. Some might tell you they're sending you your group certificate. A group certificate is exactly the

same thing as a PAYG payment summary, it's just the old name for it. Years ago, it was officially called a group certificate, and everyone's so used to calling it that that people still do today.

Example PAYG Payment Summary:

PAYG payment summary - individual non-business

Payment summary for the year ending 30 June 2012

Payee details

Mr Name McName
123 Fake Street,
Pretend Valley,
NSW, 2000

NOTICE TO PAYEE

If this payment summary shows an amount in the total tax withheld box you must lodge a tax return. If no tax was withheld you may still have to lodge a tax return.

For more information on whether you have to lodge or about this payment and how it is taxed, you can:

- visit www.ato.gov.au
- refer to *TaxPack*
- phone 13 28 61 between 8.00am and 6.00pm (EST) Monday to Friday

	Day/Month/Year		Day/Month/Year
Period of payment	01/07/2011	To	30/06/2012

Payee's tax file number   222 222 222

TOTAL TAX WITHHELD $ 4684

		Lump sum payments	Type
Gross Payments	$ 17117	A $	
CDEP Payments	$	B $	
Reportable fringe benefits amount FBT year 1 April to 31 March	$	D $	
Reportable Employer Superannuation Contributions	$	E $	
Total Allowances	$	Total allowances are not included in Gross payments above This amount needs to be shown separately in your tax return	

EXAMPLE ONLY

Payer details

Payer's ABN or withholding payer number   80 000 000 001   Branch number   123

Payer's name

Signature of authorised person   Mr Man   Date   12/11/2012

What's the difference between a PAYG Payment Summary and a payslip?
Whilst they have similar information in them, they're different summaries used for different purposes. A payslip is given to you each time you're paid, whether that's weekly, fortnightly or monthly, and it's your way of checking that you've been paid correctly for the work you've done. It's a fantastic way to see the breakdown of your wages because it lists important information:
- The hours you worked.
- Your total pay (also known as gross pay).
- The taxes taken out of that pay.
- Your final pay (also called net pay).

But it only contains information for one pay cycle. The PAYG payment summary arrives once a year and summarises the whole year, which is why it's perfect for our tax returns.

What happens if I lose it?
If you lose it, you can contact your boss or tax agent. They should have a copy they can give you. There are some copies online that only tax agents and the ATO have access to. Try to keep your copy for your own records. In the longer term, you might need your old PAYG summaries if you get audited (checked) by the ATO. That doesn't happen often, but you have to be careful. If it does happen, you'll need a lot of information and documentation to show them.

What happens if I use it incorrectly?
The only way you could use your PAYG summary incorrectly is by filling out your tax return with the wrong information from your PAYG summary. If that happens, you'll need good advice from a tax accountant about what to do. If it's a big mistake (...if it looks like you were lying to save money on tax), you might get in trouble. If it's something small, you're likely to be totally fine.

Tips and Tricks!
1) Use your payslips and PAYG summaries to check your withholding (does it seem right to you?).
2) Use your payslips and PAYG summaries to check how much you're being paid (is it correct, as promised? Can you find better paid work elsewhere?).

Update from Hayden!

Hayden used his PAYG summary to complete his tax return, but it also gave him some information about his yearly income. That helped him to make a budget.
... Once Tyler convinced him to give up his subscription to a sock delivery service.

Key Terms!

A PAYG payment summary	Your yearly wages summary.
A group certificate	Another name for a PAYG Summary.
A pay slip	Your weekly/monthly wages summary.
Before tax earnings	Your money before tax.
After tax earnings	Your money after tax.
Fringe Benefits	Things you get from work that aren't beyond your wage. For example, work might give you a car to use around the city for work.
Allowances	This is money you get from your boss for extra expenses, like if they send you to a different city and give you some money for a hotel.
Deductions from income	Money taken from your pay cheque for some reason. Maybe for a loan or child support or something similar. It's money that comes out of your pay cheque before you receive it.
Tax Withheld	Money taken to pay for your income tax.
Gross (payment)	Your total (payment), before taxes.

CHAPTER EIGHT QUIZ TIME!

1. Once the financial year is over:
   a. Your boss must send you a PAYG summary of your wages paid that year.
   b. The ATO will send you a summary your total taxes paid and how much money you have earned this year, before your return is filed.
   c. All taxes are finalised – the deadline for tax returns was before the financial year ended.
2. A PAYG Payment summary is:
   a. A summary of payments you've made to the ATO in person.
   b. A summary of your wages and all payments made to the ATO on your behalf by your employer.
   c. A summary of all payments and missed payments of taxes to the ATO.
   d. A summary of all PAYG payments made since you entered the workforce.
3. A Group Certificate is:
   a. The same thing as a PAYG Payment summary, it's just the older term for it.
   b. The same thing as a PAYG Payment summary, used in a different country.
   c. The same thing as a PAYG Payment summary, except for the whole group of employees.
   d. A totally different tax document used later on in the process.
4. You need a PAYG payment summary to...
   a. Prove you've paid precisely the tax you owe, so that no tax return is needed.
   b. To ensure you've been paid correctly by your boss, and you've received all of your holiday pay.
   c. To use the information to file a tax return.
   d. All of the above.
5. The difference between your pay slip and PAYG payment summary is that:
   a. There is no practical difference. Either can be used to file a tax return.
   b. There is no practical difference. Either can be used to check up on your employer's payments.
   c. Whilst both come at the same time, one contains more information on your wages, and the other contains more information on your taxes, and neither is used to file a return.
   d. A pay slip is given each time you receive wages, and contains information on your wages for that period, whilst the PAYG summary summaries the year's wages and tax withholding.

6. Gross and net pay are:
    a. Your before-tax-is-taken-out wage, and your after-tax-is-taken-out wage.
    b. Types of salaries depending on where you work.
    c. Impolite ways of referring to your boss.
    d. Two types of benefits received in Australia – one refers to sick pay and gross leave, and the other refers to minimum wage nets.
7. PAYG payment summaries are useful because:
    a. The ATO needs that information to calculate how much tax you were due to pay for the entirety of the year past.
    b. The ATO needs that information to confirm how much tax you've already paid.
    c. You need that information to file a tax return, so that the ATO can use the information to see how much you earned.
    d. All of the above.
8. The following documents are produced in the following order:
    a. PAYG payment summary, tax return, tax assessment.
    b. Tax assessment, PAYG payment summary, tax return.
    c. Tax return, PAYG payment summary, tax assessment.
    d. PAYG payment summary, tax assessment, tax return.

Chapter Nine:
What is a Tax Deduction?

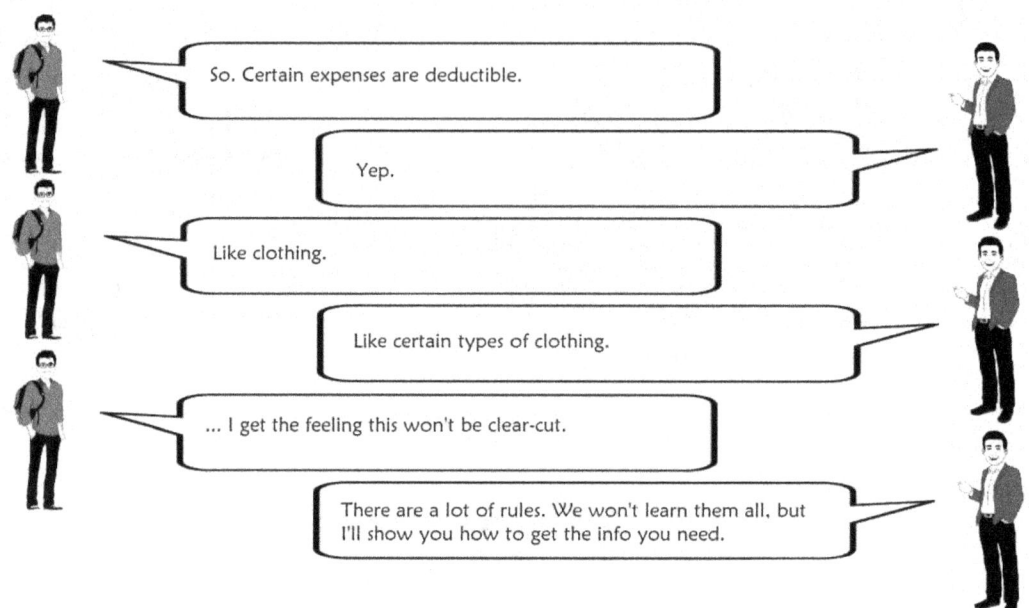

Why do I need this chapter?
This chapter explores the *what* and *how* of tax deductions.
1) What are tax deductions? How do they work?
2) Why are they important to me? How can they save me money?
3) What counts as a deduction?
4) How can I claim deductions?
5) What's the risk of claiming the wrong deductions?

> ### What is a Tax Deduction?
> A tax deduction is similar to a tax discount. When employees spend their own money on work-related expenses, they pay less tax, because their income is less.

What is a tax deduction?
When you spend the income from your job on clothes, equipment, or something else used very specifically for your job, and it's compulsory, the government doesn't think it's fair for you to pay tax on that bit of income.

That's what a tax deduction is: a reduction in tax because of work-related expenses.

Can you give me some examples, please?
Think of it in the business sense first (just to get the theory!):
If a business got $1000 from selling shirts, but spent $400 to get the shirts in the first place, then what is the real income of the business?
What's the profit?
What's taxed?

(Let's say the tax rate is 10%)

$1000 (revenue) x 10% = $100 (that would be too much tax!)
That wouldn't be fair because the business doesn't get to keep all of the $1000, so they government doesn't tax them on it.

$600 (profit: $1000-$400) x 10% = $60 (that's a fairer rate of tax)
The profit is $600, and that's what's taxed. That's $60 in tax.

The $400 they spent on shirts? That's the tax deduction.

It's similar with employees.

Let's use an example with your wages:

$500 (wages) x 10% = $50.
But you bought steel capped boots for $100, a deduction!
$400 (taxable income: $500-$100) x 10% = $40 (better!)

To really drive the point home, let's quickly use an extreme example:
You earned $500.
Your work boots cost you $500.
Really, you earned nothing. Can you imagine how it would suck if you couldn't claim your deduction? You'd still have to $50 in tax. But you don't even have any money to pay for it with.

Anyway, a deduction is the ATO's way of saying you earned less, in the end, than what your pay slips and summaries say you earned. So you pay less tax.

One more thing to note about the above calculations.
You'll notice that if you bought a pair of boots and deducted them, you saved $10 in tax in the end (in that example). You paid $100 for the boots.

There's a common misconception that work expenses are free because you get the full amount back in your tax refund. It's not true. They're not free, they're *tax free*. In the end, you save some tax money, but you don't get the full cost of the deduction back. Remember that!

So... How do I do this 'tax deduction' stuff, then?
First off, you don't get the reduction in tax until the end of the financial year.
You get it by listing the deduction (the expense) in your tax return. By doing this, you are reducing your income in the eyes of the tax office. And the lower your income is, the less tax you'll pay.

Remember, as you've already paid your taxes in withholding, what that means is you'll get more tax back in your refund at the end of the year.

Oh, and *keep your receipts*! Otherwise you might not be able to claim the deduction!

What is tax deductible?
Whilst it's exciting to think you can get larger tax refunds, I'm sorry to say that not every single thing you buy can be listed as a tax deduction. There are rules that determine what you can deduct. You can't deduct the cost of everything from your gym membership to your hair product. The most important rule is that the items *have to be used specifically and necessarily for work*. And even then, it can be hard to find valid deductions!

There are a lot of rules about tax deductions, so if you're not sure what's valid and what isn't, keep all your receipts and give them to your tax agent if you have one. He'll be able to help you figure it out. If you don't have one, you'll have to do the research yourself, by using the ATO website and calling them.

I can try to give you some help in this book, but there are simply too many variations on jobs and situations for me to be comprehensive, so all I can do is give you *general advice*!

Three Rules for Deductions:
1) You must have spent the money yourself (you weren't reimbursed!).
2) It must be directly related to earning your income.
3) You must have a record to prove it.

Even then, the expense might not be deductible. For example, just because you bought a pair of pants for work doesn't necessarily mean they're deductible. They

have to be really specific to your job. For example, if a chef has those checked black-and-white pants that only a chef wears.
He's not going to wear those in his day-to-day life.
They're deductible.

Online, the ATO has industry-specific lists of potential deductions. That's a good place to start to learn what you might be able to claim. They also have fact sheets that give you more information.

Deductions: do I have to do them?
Are you kidding? Well no, you don't *have to* list them in your tax return. But it's your money! You could get a larger tax refund at the end of the financial year if you're just careful and take good notes and keep good records during the year.
Many, many people lose out on money every year because they are lazy or just don't understand the system. Don't be one of them! Be careful to note down your deductions.

Are there any risks with tax deductions?
Sure: claiming things you shouldn't claim. My advice is to check with the ATO and your accountant, and be honest with yourself.

Tips and Tricks!
1) Keep your receipts! Generally, for five years! (The government could ask for proof of your deductions at any time)
2) Do your research about what's deductable and what isn't.
3) Be honest.
4) Use the government's MyDeductions app!
5) Read up about deductions on the ATO website.
6) Don't go on a shopping spree for deductions! For two reasons:
    a. Remember, work expenses are income-tax-free, not totally free.
    b. If you have the choice to buy them or not buy them, they're probably not "necessary for work".

Update from Hayden!

Hayden started thinking about all the money he's spent on his job. The union fees, the uniform laundry costs... Actually, that's everything he spent that was directly related to work. So he wrote them down, found the receipts and kept them, and now he can claim them when the time comes to file a tax return!

Key Terms!
Tax deduction   A suitable work-related expense.

That's all folks!

CHAPTER NINE QUIZ TIME!

1. What is a tax deduction?
    a. A reduction in the amount of tax you pay because of your living conditions.
    b. An expense – something you bought that you needed specifically for work. It means you pay less tax.
    c. The tax deducted from your pay check and sent to the ATO as withholding taxes.
    d. A voluntary payment of your taxes, paid as you buy something at a store, instead of paying the taxes through your employer.
2. What's the point of a tax deduction?
    a. To make allowances for the costs of being employed, therefore making tax fairer.
    b. To give more flexibility in the payment of taxes.
    c. To keep taxation low in Australia.
    d. To keep taxation low in Australia for certain minority groups.
    e. All of the above.
3. Which of the following would you think are tax deductible expenses for someone who works on a construction site?
    a. A hardhat, as required for the person's safety.
    b. The underwear he wears every day.
    c. General costs of living like the home electricity bill.
    d. Both A and B.
4. In the eyes of the ATO, claiming a tax-deductible expense:
    a. Lowers your income, because the ATO doesn't want to tax you on money you didn't keep for yourself.
    b. Increases your income, so the ATO can balance out what you earned after what you had to spend on work expenses.
    c. Is only possible if you are over 18.
5. You bought some safety shoes that your job requires you to buy. You:
    a. Do nothing, as they are not a tax deduction.
    b. Tell the tax office immediately, and send them your receipt for the purchase.
    c. Send a bill to your boss, as it is a work expense.
    d. Keep the receipt until the end of the financial year, and list the shoes as a deduction in your tax return.
6. Forgetting to list a tax deduction is bad because:
    a. You lose some money when you receive your tax refund.
    b. You could get in trouble with the ATO.
    c. You could be fined for not listing your deductions.

    d. It's a good thing, because it means you don't have to pay for the deduction.
7. The more deductions you have:
    a. The lower your income is, and the higher your refund will be.
    b. The higher your income is, and therefore the higher your refund will be.
    c. It will have no effect on your refund.
    d. The less tax you'll have to pay next financial year.
8. I need to keep my receipts:
    a. I don't need to keep the receipt as long as I copy down the information from it.
    b. To prove my deductions were real.
    c. Because the receipt will tell me if the good I bought is tax deductible or not – it's always written beneath the total.
    d. All of the above.
9. A tax agent:
    a. Cannot help you find your possible deductions.
    b. Guarantees you won't miss out on any deductions, ever.
    c. Will help you find as many deductions as possible.
    d. Will help you stop claiming deductions, so that you will get a higher refund.
10. The best way to keep your receipts is to:
    a. Put them somewhere safe and sound, neat and tidy so that they can be easily used for your tax return at the end of the financial year.
    b. Give them to your tax agent piece by piece.
    c. Leave them under your pillow, so the tax fairy will give you your refund while you sleep.
    d. It doesn't really matter. I'm busy. A good tax agent will be able to figure the whole thing out later.

Chapter Ten:
What is a Tax Return?

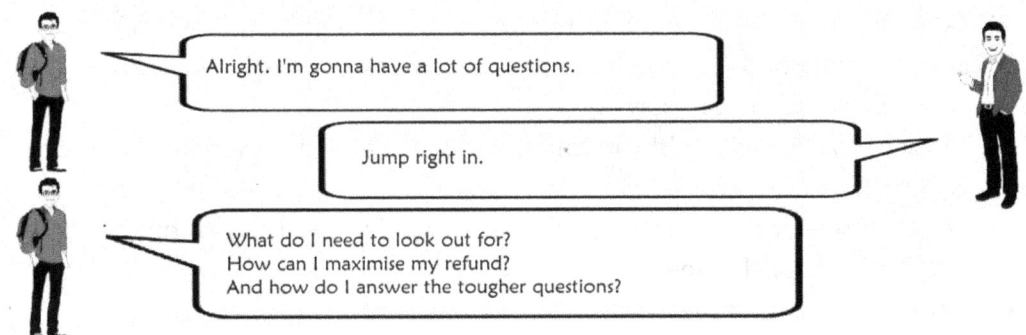

Why do I need this chapter?
This chapter explores the *what* and *how* of tax returns.
1) What is a tax return?
2) What's in a tax return?
3) What are the different ways of filing a tax return?
4) What is a tax agent?
5) What are the risks and benefits of filing a tax return?
6) How can I get a larger tax refund?
7) When is my tax return due?

> *What Is a Tax Return?*
> A tax return is a document that a tax payer and/or his account prepares and gives to the tax office. It has information about that person's income, used by the ATO to calculate the tax due to be paid or refunded.

What is a tax return?
When the financial year ends, you've earned a lot of money.
You've also already paid a lot in tax.
But still, no one is quite sure how much tax you were *supposed* to have paid for the year. That's where a tax return comes in handy. You put a bunch of information in it about your income and financial situation, and the ATO calculates the rest.

A tax return is your summary of the year past, created to settle tax affairs for that time period.

What's in a tax return?
No matter how they're filed, via an accountant or online, or in some other way, tax returns cover the same stuff. Tax returns are used by the ATO to create a tax assessment. Below are some things they need to know:
1) Who you are (with the help of a tax file number).
2) What kinds of income you had (a job, shares, multiple houses etc)
3) What you earned (by totalling up all earnings from PAYG Payment summaries and other sources).
4) How much tax you paid (by totalling PAYG Payment summaries and other records).
5) What offsets or deductions you're claiming (by totalling up the receipts you've kept for the year).
6) And a good deal more!

How can I complete and lodge a tax return?
Tax returns require you to answer a lot of really specific questions accurately. Most people struggle with their tax returns, which is why many, many people hire a tax agent. Does everyone have to have one? No, people can and do complete their own tax returns. You have essentially three choices when it comes to completing your tax return:
1) Use an online tax agent.
2) See a tax agent in person, at an office.
3) Complete the tax return yourself online.

You used to be able to complete your tax return offline with paper and pen, but the ATO phased it out.

What is a tax agent and how can I use one?
A tax agent is any licensed person who can lodge your tax return for you. Whether you use an online one or a real-life face-to-face accountant, you have many companies to choose from, and a large price range. A Google search will show you the major competitors.

For full information on tax agents and accountants, see the next chapter.

What's the difference between online and real-life accountants?
Real-life accountants are good because they'll sit you down and talk you through the whole process. It's an incredible opportunity to ask all the questions you want (so long as you have a patient accountant) and learn a lot about the system and how to maximise your return and look after your own interests.

Online tax return services will charge a fee in exchange for their help. Make sure you do your research and choose a site you want to use, at the rate you want to pay. Many people choose online tax agents. They're often simple and fast, PLUS, you get the added extra of having an accountant check over your return from cyber space. Or at least some pointers and tips to maximise your return as you go through the process.

How much work these online accountants actually do, and exactly how much value-for-money you get, is debateable. Many people think you simply don't your money's worth in comparison to the ATO's *myTax*.

How can I complete and lodge my return myself? What's "myTax"?

The ATO provides resources for people who choose to lodge their returns themselves:

1) Online tax-return lodgement services, myTax (log onto the site, go through their lodgement process, and voila, your return is done).
2) Fact sheets, videos and calculators to offer you information.
3) A phone service to answer your questions.

MyTax is the ATO's free downloadable tax software. Because it's free, you won't receive the help of an accountant or tax agent, but you do have access to the ATO website which is full of fact sheets and information, as well as the ATO's phone helpline.

Does anyone use the tax pack anymore?

The tax pack is a paper-and-pen version of a tax return. It's something the ATO has provided free of charge for people who don't want to use a computer, or a tax agent. It's very unpopular now. The ATO phased it out now that we have the internet.

What's myGov, by the way?

myGov is another government thing. MyGov is the online filing system/website the government uses for ALL your important record, designed for you to use. That includes tax stuff, Medicare stuff, Centrelink stuff, all that. It's pretty handy to have it all in one place.

With a simple internet search you can find myGov, and you can follow the prompts to login and use it!

When is my tax return due?
Remember your deadlines for your taxes! As soon as the financial year ends on July 1st, you'll start receiving documents from employers to help you lodge. You have four months to get your return in – the deadline is **October 31st**: Halloween!

What if I'm late submitting my tax return?
Often, nothing will happen straight away. Usually, it's your money going to waste, so the tax office isn't in a hurry to force you to lodge (why, when they can just keep your money for themselves?). But, they sometimes fine people for being late! They send you a warning first, then fine you if you still don't complete it.

Are tax returns complex?
Yes. And no.
For most people, taxation is an on-going learning experience that lasts their entire lives. This book can teach you the basics and where to go for help, but there is only so much it can explain in one go. It can't walk you through your tax return because they're long and diverse - there's too much that changes for each person. That's why a tax agent is so useful.

A tax agent is there to help you. A good tax agent doesn't mind taking a moment to explain the things that you don't understand. This stuff gets confusing, and really boring. But if you hire a tax agent, you almost don't have to worry. A good tax agent will do the whole thing, do it properly, and do it with your best interests in mind.

What are the benefits of filing a tax return?
In short, there are two big reasons and several small reasons to file, and file on time:
1) You'll probably get a tax refund (yessss, money for you!).
2) You won't be at risk of a fine/getting in trouble for not completing your tax return.

It's also just good to be organised, prepared, and prudent in dry, functional stuff like this. Tax is one of those things that get harder the longer you leave them. With every passing month and even year, you lose more records and proofs, and you lose motivation to get it done.

Also, having your records is useful. Tax records can be used as proof address or employment, and doing the work encourages a prepared, empowered lifestyle.

Don't forget, you have a legal requirement to complete your tax return before the deadline and to meet the ATO's requirements. Many people still don't. Every year, the ATO's auditors are working hard to catch people out.

What can go wrong when filing a tax return?
1) You might make some errors. Maybe you realise only after you lodge. If that happens, see a tax agent. You may have to lodge an amendment.
2) You could get taken advantage of by an dishonest tax agent. This happens! Be careful, and make sure the company and person is reputable. The way to do that is to check that the company is large with many happy customers.
3) You could lie. Don't do that. It's not worth it. You'll have to pay the money back, plus fines and interest.

How can I get a larger refund and pay less tax?
Here are some things you can do to maximise your refund and reduce your tax:
1) Carefully list and keep records of all deductions.
2) Tick the 'claim tax-free threshold' box on your TFN declaration form to avoid overpaying in taxes each pay cheque (for one job only!).
3) Keep an eye out for any tax offsets that might be available to you. Usually, these are only in specific or difficult situations, like caring for a disabled person in your home, but a tax agent will be able to inform you properly of anything specific to you.

Tips and Tricks!
1) See the 'how can I save money' section for some awesome ways to pay less tax.
2) See knowledgeable people if you need advice (your tax agent, the ATO).
3) If your parents are good with money, try filing your tax return in the same way as them for your first one. That way you have somewhere to start and can ask questions.
4) If you're going to an accountant, shop around for a good one your trust with a fair price.

Update from Hayden:

Hayden tried filing his own taxes at first with the ATO's myTax program. He liked it, but he was worried about a few specific things about his tax situation. His parents recommended a good accountant, and he went into their office with some questions to ask. He found an accountant he liked, he asked a bunch of questions, and he now feels a lot more comfortable about his taxes.

Important Key Terms!

Tax return	A document you give to the ATO with information about your earnings and the year passed.
Tax Agent	An accountant who helps you file your return.
myTax	The government's program that you can use to lodge your return for free.
myGov	A government site that links a lot of your public services into one, like tax and welfare.
Online tax agent	A tax agent from cyber space that you may never meet.
Real-life tax agent	A tax agent with an office you can visit.
File/Lodge	Both these words mean the same thing. They are verbs for when you give your return to the tax office.

Example Tax Return:

Here are some pages from an example tax return, so you can see what they look like. Different accountants and software systems might make them look different, but in the end, all tax returns are the same: a long document with information about you and the year passed.

This tax return was 33 pages long. Here are just some of those pages.

Tax return for individuals 2012

1 July 2011 to 30 June 2012

Australian Government
Australian Taxation Office

Your tax file number (TFN) [blank] — See the Privacy note in the *Taxpayer's declaration* on page 12 of your tax return.

Are you an Australian resident? YES [X] NO [ ]

Your sex Male [X] Female [ ]

Your name
Print your full name.
Title – for example, Mr, Mrs, Ms, Miss: Mr
Surname or family name: [blank]
Given names: [blank]

Has any part of your name changed since completing your last tax return? NO [X] YES [ ]
Previous surname: [blank]

Your postal address
Print the address where you want your mail sent.
[blank]
Suburb / town / locality: [blank]
State / territory: [blank] Postcode: [blank] Country if not Australia: [blank]

Has this address changed since completing your last tax return? Fill in the appropriate box then read on. NO [X] YES [ ]

Is your home address different from your postal address? NO [X] Read on. YES [ ] Print your home address.
Suburb / town / locality: [blank]
State / territory: [blank] Postcode: [blank] Country if not Australia: [blank]

Your date of birth
If you were under 18 years old on 30 June 2012 you must complete item A1 on page 7.
DAY MONTH YEAR [blank] — Provide your date of birth to avoid delays in the processing of your tax return.

Your phone number during business hours – If we need to ask you about your tax return, it is quicker by phone.
Area code: 04 Telephone number: [blank]

Will you need to lodge an Australian tax return in the future? YES [X] DON'T KNOW [ ] NO [ ] FINAL TAX RETURN [ ]

IN CONFIDENCE - when completed

Lodgment Ref No: [blank] 1

Mind the Gap

Electronic funds transfer (EFT)
Provide your financial institution details.
Write the BSB number, account number and account name below.

BSB number (must be six digits) [ ] Account number [ ]

Account name (for example, JQ Citizen. Do not show the account type, such as cheque, savings, mortgage offset)
[ ]

INCOME

1 Salary or wages — Your main salary and wage occupation [ ]

Payer's Australian business number	Tax withheld – do not show cents		Income – do not show cents	
		.00	C	.00
		.00	D	.00
		.00	E	.00
		.00	F	.00
		.00	G	.00

2 Allowances, earnings, tips, director's fees etc [ ] .00   K [ ] .00

3 Employer lump sum payments
Amount A in lump sum payments box — TYPE
[ ] .00   R [ ] .00 [ ]
5% of amount B in lump sum payments box
[ ] .00   H [ ] .00

4 Employment termination payments (ETP)
Date of payment   Day Month Year
Payer's ABN [ ]
Taxable component   TYPE
[ ] .00   I [ ] .00 [ ]

5 Australian Government allowances and payments like Newstart, Youth Allowance and Austudy payment [ ] .00   A [ ] .00

6 Australian Government pensions and allowances
You must also complete item T2 or T3 in Tax offsets.
[ ] .00   B [ ] .00

7 Australian annuities and superannuation income streams [ ] .00
Taxable component   Taxed element   J [ ] .00
Untaxed element   N [ ] .00
Lump sum in arrears – taxable component   Taxed element   Y [ ] .00
Untaxed element   Z [ ] .00

8 Australian superannuation lump sum payments [ ] .00   TYPE [ ]
Date of payment   Day Month Year
Payer's ABN [ ]
Taxable component   Taxed element   Q [ ] .00
Untaxed element   P [ ] .00

9 Attributed personal services income [ ] .00   O [ ] .00

TOTAL TAX WITHHELD $ [ ] .00 ← For items 1 to 9 add up all the amounts in the tax withheld column.

IN CONFIDENCE - when completed   **Lodgment Ref No:** [ ]

Mind the Gap

Taxpayer Name: ▮
Tax File Number: ▮
Signature: ....

Gross interest

Description	Your share TFN amounts withheld (less any refunded)	Your share of gross interest

Total
* The cent values will not be displayed on your tax return.

Dividends

Entity description	Your share unfranked amount	Your share franked amount	Your share franking credits	Your share TFN withheld

* The cent values will not be displayed on your tax return.

Work related uniform, clothing and laundry

Description of expenses	Amount claimed

Total

Work-related self-education expenses – general expenses

Description of expenses	Amount claimed

Total

Work-related self-education expenses – decline in value of depreciating assets

Description of expenses	Amount claimed

Total

Work-related self-education expenses – general expenses not allowable as a deduction

Description of expenses	Amount claimed

Total

Other work related expenses

Description of expenses	Amount claimed

Total

Net medical expenses

Description	Gross amount	Refundable amount	Net medical expense

Total

Retain this page for your records - the information on this page is NOT sent to the ATO

CHAPTER TEN QUIZ TIME!
1. Who can file your tax return?
    a. You.
    b. A tax agent.
    c. The ATO.
    d. Either A or B.
    e. Any of the above.
2. Tax returns can be completed:
    a. Online, or through your boss.
    b. Online, or through Centrelink.
    c. Online, or with an accountant.
    d. In person at your local politician's office.
3. Tax agents:
    a. Are required by law.
    b. Are only available immediately after the financial year.
    c. Are recommended for those who are not tax experts.
    d. Are not recommended, as they do not know your private matters. It's best to file your own return.
4. A tax return is used by:
    a. The ATO, to produce a PAYG payment summary and therefore a potential refund.
    b. Your boss, to pay your taxes to the ATO.
    c. The ATO, to produce a tax assessment and therefore a potential refund.
    d. You, to complete your tax assessment before sending it off to the ATO.
5. The purpose of a tax return is to:
    a. Give the ATO information on your income, taxes, and other personal information to produce a tax assessment.
    b. Tell you, as the tax payer, what the tax requirements are for you for that particular financial year.
    c. Pay your taxes ahead of time, because it's safer.
    d. Revisit old tax files to look for errors, mistakes or frauds.
6. To complete a tax return, you need:
    a. Your PAYG payment summaries.
    b. A list of your deductions.
    c. Your Tax File Number.
    d. All of the above.

7. Filing your tax return is important because:
    a. Without doing so, you won't get a tax refund if one is due to you.
    b. You could get in trouble for not filing.
    c. All your friends are doing it, and you don't want to seem irresponsible.
    d. A, B and maybe C are all true.

Chapter Eleven: What is a Tax Agent?

So, what are my options?

Why do I need this chapter?
This chapter explores the *what*, *how* and *how much* of tax agents.
1) What is a tax agent?
2) What's the difference between a tax agent and an accountant?
3) Why should I use a tax agent? What are the benefits?
4) Where can I find a tax agent?
5) Who can be a tax agent?
6) What are the different types of tax agents and services?
7) How much should I pay for a tax agent?
8) What are the risks of using a tax agent?
9) What is self-assessment?
10) What do I give to my tax agent?

What is a Tax Agent?
A tax agent is a professional who represents their client in tax matters. They help the client to complete and lodge their tax return in the best interests of the client, and advises their client.

What is a tax agent?
In short, a tax agent helps you file your tax return.

They might be an individual or a large company. They have qualifications and experience in the accounting and taxation world, and have the correct qualifications and certifications to complete the work. They are your representative, so they can make decisions and act on your behalf. For example, they can apply for an extension to your tax return deadline for you.

What's the difference between a tax agent and an accountant?
These two things are almost the same.

"Accountant" is a general term. An accountant is any person who works with financial numbers. That could be with a large company, doing payroll or bills for example, but not necessarily with tax and tax returns. A tax agent specifically is a person who helps individuals lodge their returns.

All tax agents are accountants.

Not all accountants are tax agents.

Why should I use a tax agent?
A tax agent is a professional at maximising your refund, which means that they often do a better job of getting you more money back than you would do yourself. They promote themselves by saying that people will save more money with them than they would doing it on their own.

But how can you save money when you're spending all that money on the accountant in the first place?

They often suggest that the extra refund you get is going to be bigger than the cost of paying for the tax agent. For example, if the accountant costs you $200, and you get a refund worth $300 MORE than you would have otherwise got, it's a good deal, right?

One possible example:
Tax refund without tax agent: $500
Tax refund with tax agent: $800
Cost of tax agent: $200

Sometimes it works out that way, it IS a good deal.

It often doesn't, as well. Sometimes they get you back an extra $100, but they cost you the same $200 for their services. Also sometimes they get you back the same amount you would have received anyway, if you had done it yourself!

The more complex your tax situation, the more chance there is that an accountant will be able to help you out in a big way, and save you big dollars.

A tax agent can't guarantee you a better refund, especially without looking at your situation. It all depends on your situation and how good you are at your taxes.

The simpler the return, the less need you'll have for an accountant.

Here are some benefits of using a tax agent:
1) You might save money.
2) You save all the time, worry and confusion of trying to do it yourself.
3) You get personal tax advice, so you get all the help you need and you can learn all about this stuff at the same time.
4) You're less likely to get in trouble for doing the return wrong, because the tax agent is a professional and knows what he's doing.
5) A tax agent is your representative, so they can ask the ATO for an extension on your return if you're running late submitting it.

It's handy to have a tax agent. They're kind of like your tax defender. If you get a good one, they'll take good care of you. It's cool also to keep the same agent for a long time. They get to know you and your situation, and you have a point of reference with them: someone to ask questions if there's something you don't understand.

Where can I find a tax agent?
You can find tax agents with a bit of research. Try the following areas:
1) Online.
2) You might see their offices around your city/town with other shops.
3) Shopping centres even sometimes have them set up temporarily at tax time.
4) Word of mouth (family and friends might recommend a good one).
Remember to check that they're reputable and legal!
Only a registered tax agent is allowed to take your money to help you. See below!

Who can be a tax agent?
Not just anyone can be a tax agent. You have to be certified, qualified, checked and registered by the authority. As mentioned above, you can check if your accountant has the legal ability to complete your return: you can check the register with the Tax Practitioner's Board. Just type in their business name, and they should come up.

If you're interested in becoming an accountant yourself, I'd recommend an accounting degree.

What are the different types of tax agents and services?
There are two main types of tax agent you'll find: online and real-world.

The online world can be a little difficult to navigate. There are various services that assist you with lodging a tax return for a fee. Many of them provide a flashy alternative to the government's online program, myTax. Some might have better, simpler layouts, solid explanations and resources, and personal assistance. Some are good, some are not.

Some companies try to act as though they are a government program, not an independent and for-profit company, which they are. Then there are people pretending to be tax agents that just aren't. You can lose a lot of money through scammers in the tax system, so be careful!

It's not always easy to know what's a government program (like myTax), what's a private company (like an online tax agent), and what's a scam.
Try the following:
1) Check if they charge money. Private companies charge money. The government offers free resources. With government stuff, you shouldn't have to give credit card details.
2) Stuff from the government usually has the government of Australia or ATO logo on it (still not fool-proof, there are copy-and-pasters out there)!
3) Check the URL (website address).
4) Check online reviews (from OTHER sites, other URLs).
5) Check with people you trust.
6) Check the Tax Practitioners' Board website for their registration.
7) Check that the company operates in Australia.
8) Use your intuition –
   a. Do they make big promises that are too good to be true?
   b. Are they asking for information they don't need, or
   c. Asking for it at the wrong time (credit card details first)?
   d. Do they seem professional/does it feel right?

If the internet's not your style, what's your other option? You can visit a tax agent in person, with a real office, and you can sit with them while they answer all your questions. Everyone has different preferences, and whatever works for you, works for you.

How much should I pay for a tax agent?

A prudent person will browse around and ask for quotes for a tax return. They will also take into account the how reputable the business is.
1) Do they present well and seem professional?
2) Are they friendly and open with you?
3) Are their fees easy to understand?
4) Do they seem knowledgeable?
5) Have they been around long?
6) How large is the company?
7) Have you read any reviews of the company?
8) Does anyone you know use them?
9) Are they registered with the Tax Practitioners' Board?

Once you take into account these elements, a normal tax return could cost you anywhere from **$80 to $300** for the most simple ones. The more complicated the tax return, the more it will cost! It might seem like a lot, and it is. But it's helping you with something really important: your financial wellbeing.

Some accountants take their fees out of the refund, so you don't have to pay anything up front.

Oh, don't forget! Make sure you look carefully over the work they do, and ask good questions to make sure it makes sense and is correct.

What are the risks of using a tax agent, and what is self-assessment?

Using a tax agent doesn't mean that nothing will go wrong, though it helps. Apart from choosing a dodgy accountant, the main risk is still you. You still can't give wrong information: your accountant won't take the blame if you've lied or forgotten something important. You can still get in trouble.

In Australia, we have something called "self-assessment". Self-assessment is the policy that it's up to you to make sure that the information you give is true. You are responsible for submitting a return with the correct information, even if a tax agent helps you with it. If the ATO comes and checks on you, they will be very thorough, and they can be very harsh.

What do I give to my tax agent?
Here are some things your tax agent might ask for:
- Your PAYG payment summary.
- Your tax file number.
- Details of any investments or other incomes.
- A list of your deductions (if you have any).
- Bank account information (for them to pay your refund, if you get one).

They are likely to ask you a lot of questions about your current situation to try to find the best way for you to save money.

Tips and Tricks!
1) Choose a patient, friendly accountant that you like and trust. That way, you will feel more comfortable asking questions and learning. Check reviews online before you finalise your choice!
2) Check that your tax agent is registered with the Tax Practitioners' Board.
3) Get your tax agent to quote both their fee and your refund.
4) If you're chatting with a tax agent, take it slow! If they ask you a bunch of questions you don't understand, ask them to explain.
5) If you're submitting your tax return online, research the website you're using and look online for reviews (external to the site).
6) When you're filing out documents, make a list of questions or things you're not sure about. You can ask someone like a tax agent, your parents, or the ATO.
7) It's allllll about organisation. Make your life easier – keep your documents and information sorted carefully by financial year as you go along! And keep it all in one place! Otherwise it'll be a big task to sort it out when your tax agent asks.
8) Don't put it off! If you leave it until tomorrow, it'll feel worse to start again than to finish in the first place.

Your tax return is often the most tedious part.
But really, it's not so bad. All that you have to do is keep some documents (your PAYG summary, any bank or investment stuff, deductions stuff, etc), then hand them over to a professional. That's it.

You'll get faster over the years.

Update from Hayden!

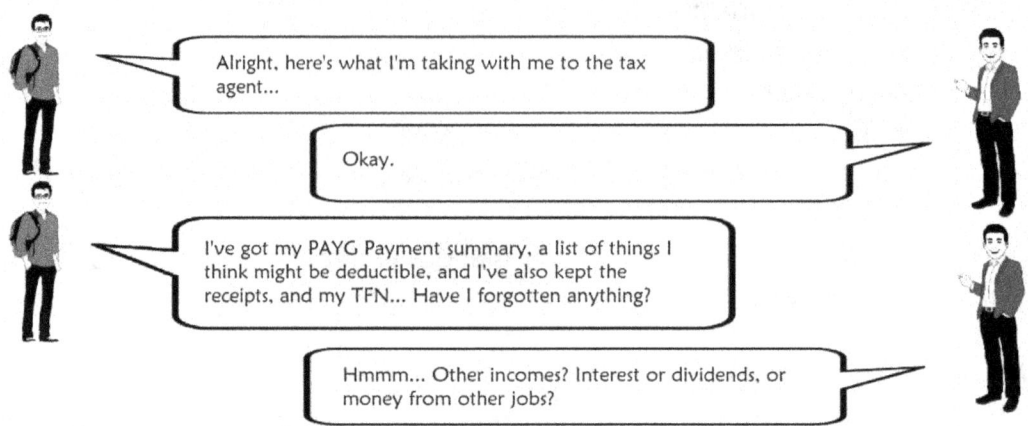

Hayden had actually been quite careful over the course of the year and had his documents in one folder in his room. He managed to get everything in and his tax return was completed pretty fast.

Key Terms!
Accountant	A person who works with financial numbers.
Tax Agent	An accountant that work with taxes and tax returns.
Self-assessment	A policy from the government: the responsibility is yours to supply correct information, and you could get in trouble if you don't.

CHAPTER ELEVEN QUIZ TIME!

1. What is a tax agent?
    a. Someone who organises your tax withholding.
    b. Someone who prepares your tax assessment.
    c. Someone who prepares your tax return.
    d. All of the above.
2. What can a tax agent help you with?
    a. Preparing your tax return, preparing your tax refund, and withholding your taxes.
    b. Preparing your tax return, finding potential tax deductions and giving tax advice.
    c. Preparing your tax return, deducting things not related to work, and defending you in court.
    d. Giving tax advice, preparing your return, and choosing a cheap tax file number.
3. Why might a tax agent be worth the fees you pay?
    a. To save time, hassle, and tax money.
    b. Because a tax agent never ever makes a mistake, which is good.
    c. Because it gives you the freedom to commit tax fraud and blame it on someone else.
    d. It's never worth it. Even though I'm not very good with tax stuff, I don't want to seek out help.
4. What's the difference between a tax agent and an accountant?
    a. An accountant adds up your taxes, and the tax agent presents it to the tax office.
    b. The tax agent works for the tax office, and the accountant does not.
    c. The tax agent is the accountant's representative.
    d. A tax agent is a type of accountant that represents you in your tax affairs.
5. Some extra things a tax agent can do for you are:
    a. Give you sound tax advice.
    b. Help you collect lost receipts if you can't find them.
    c. Keep good records for you, like store all your summaries, notices, and receipts at his office year-round.
    d. All of the above.
6. If I don't want to use a tax agent, I can:
    a. Complete my return myself online.
    b. Not complete one and assume everything will work out fine.

    c. Complete it myself, but that's very unusual and there are really not many resources out there to help me.
    d. Submit a non-agent return, which is a simpler return that allows for some mistakes.
7. Which of the below is the best option of good things to give to your tax agent, so that he can complete your return?
    a. My boss's phone number, a list of the hours I worked, and at least one pay slip.
    b. Last year's tax return alone is enough for the tax agent.
    c. A list of deductions, all my PAYG summaries and my tax file number.
    d. My tax file number, my receipts and all of the past returns my family has completed.
8. How can I get the most from my tax agent?
    a. Find an agent that specialises in your type of tax return, and organise all of your paperwork really well, including having a list of questions to ask the agent.
    b. Don't keep any documentation during the year and expect the agent to solve all of your problems.
    c. Show up at the appointment without really thinking about what you need to bring and what you need to ask, get really confused about what is really required, and then leave the office to get the documents but never come back.

Chapter Twelve: How Do I Use MyTax?

> MyTax is a great tool. It doesn't offer personal advice, but for a simple return, it might be a good option.

Why do I need this chapter?
This chapter explains the *what* and *how* of MyTax.
1) What is MyTax?
2) What are the pros and cons of MyTax?
3) How do I use it?

What is MyTax?
My tax is a free option for people to lodge their tax returns.
It's provided online by the ATO.

What are the pros and cons of using MyTax?
Pros:
1) It's free.
2) It's online.
3) It's easy-ish to use.
4) It's relatively fast.

Cons:
1) It doesn't offer advice from a tax professional.

How do I use it?
Some notes before I begin!
1) This chapter was written in early 2018. MyTax may have changed.
2) This information is meant for general employees who are younger and who have simpler tax situations. It wasn't written for people who earn money in other interesting ways, like operating as a sole trader (finding some work yourself from a customer, not working for a boss from inside a company).
3) Just another friendly reminder: this is general advice, not personal advice for your situation. I'll do my best to show you what stuff means, but you have to make choices that are best for you and your situation. Or use a tax

professional.

So.
MyTax.
It's easy to use. A lot of it is self-explanatory. For the more difficult questions, potentially confusing questions, I've lent some suggestions below.

What is Pre-filling?
Here's some more good news: you can pre-fill a lot of information.
"Pre-filling" is where the system takes the information from somewhere else, like the ATO's records. This includes MyDeductions – the ATO app for you to use throughout the year to record your expenses. Try it out!
It means you don't have to find the information yourself and type it in: it's already done.

Be careful though! Just because MyTax prefills the information, does not mean that it's correct or complete. You have to check it very carefully.

How can I find MyTax?
A simple Google search will get it in front of you.
You can also find it in your MyGov account – where a lot of your government related stuff is (Centrelink, Medicare, Taxes...).

How does it work?
MyTax is you working directly with the ATO, no tax agent intermediary.

MyTax is split into four steps:
1) Contact Details (who are you?)
2) Financial Institution Details (your bank, so they can pay you your refund!)
3) Personalise Return (what kind of return do you need?)
4) Prepare Return (fill in the blanks and make your return)

Let's get started!

Personalise Your Return!
Personalise your return: tax resident
"Were you an Australian resident for tax purposes from 1 July ____ to June 30 ____?"

If you lived in Australia for the whole of the last financial year, then you almost certainly were a resident for tax purposes. If you have any reason to suspect otherwise (you lived and worked overseas during this time, for example), call the ATO to confirm.

If you're in Australia on a visa, remember: they are not asking you if you are a permanent resident in your visa status. Being a resident for tax purposes is different.

Personalise your return: salary and wages
Here, you're ticking the box of what kind of money you've received this year. The PAYG summaries that you boss(es) sent you in the post are a good place to start.

Please remember!
People can have several summaries. Your return might have been pre-filled with your PAYG summary(s), but they might not ALL be there. They can be left off the pre-filling process sometimes.
And even your boss could fail to get your summary to you for whatever reason. Think back: what were all your the incomes for that financial year? Check that they are all there!

Also remember! These are incomes. Money you receive. Not expenses (don't tick the rent box unless you own a house you rented to someone else and got money for it!)

Personalise your return: salary

Salary/wages	Your normal pay check.
Government payments	Centrelink payments.
Employment termination	If you lost your job and got extra money.
Foreign employment	If you worked overseas.
Attributed Personal Services	Income from work for your extra efforts, beyond your usual wages and overtime. Like a kind of bonus. It'd be on your summary.

Personalise your return: super or annuity
Super income is for when you're retired and you took money out of your super to live on. Unless you've taken money out of your super, don't tick this box.

Annuity is a special kind of investment. You will probably know if you have one. Most young adults don't. If you're not sure if do, you'll need to look carefully through your records or contact any financial institutions you've worked with that might know.

Personalise your return: interest or investments
This section includes interest from bank accounts, and anything to do with owning houses or shares on the stock market. Is this you?

Interest	Money your bank gives you for storing money with them.
Dividends	Payments from shares (from that company's profits!).
Rent	Owning a house and renting it out.
Managed Funds	Shares again, but a special kind.
Capital Gains	If you sold something big for more than you paid for it – like some shares.
Capital Losses	If you sold something big for less than you paid for it.

Personalise your return: sole trader
Do you have an ABN (see other MTG resources!)?
Have you earned money running a business of your own?

Personalise your return: deductions
Tick the box for the correct type!
I hope you have your list of deductions ready: maybe you've been keeping careful track all year long?

Personalise your return: offsets
These rarely apply to a simple return for a young person.

Prepare Your Return!
Prepare your return: payment summaries
Check that ALL your incomes are here. For each and every job, even if you were only paid for one hour of work (I'm serious!).

If there's something missing from pre-filling, you can add it in yourself. Just put in the numbers from your PAYG summary(s).

Prepare your return: interest
If you keep money in a bank account, your bank might pay you to keep it there.

That's called interest. You'd need a fair amount of money in a high-interest bank account to have any significant interest.

It might seem crazy, but if you earned money (any money) in interest, it's taxable. It's an income!

If you gave your TFN to your bank, they'll take care of it for you. It should already be entered into the system (pre-filled). If you didn't, you'll have to get a summary of your interest earnings for the year!
Give your bank a call. They'll help you.

Prepare your return: deductions
Alright, here we go! Deductions!
You're doing your tax return yourself, so you'd better be sure those deductions are valid (or the ATO might end up hunting you down, four years from now). On the ATO website, there are lists of acceptable deductions for each type of job.
That's pretty cool. Use that.

Prepare your return: income tests
This is where you can list some information to see if you're valid for any offsets. The ordinary teenager isn't, but you have to make sure the information listed is correct.

Fringe Benefits	Sometimes , people get more than money from their boss. They might get support with rent, or a car to use. List those here. Check with the ATO to make sure it's an official fringe benefit!
Government Pensions	Get any money for being old? Old people sometimes get money from the government to help them. Probably not you, though. Right?
Investment Loss	Any bad stock market investments?
Child support	Did you have to pay your ex-partner to support your child?
Super contributions	Did you pay extra money into your superannuation?
Foreign income	Did you earn money overseas?
Property loss	Do you own properties, and lose money on them?
Dependent children	How many children do you take care of?

For many, if not most teenagers and young adults, all of those numbers will be zero.

Prepare your return: Medicare and private health insurance

Medicare is the government organisation that helps keep hospitals and doctors free, or cheaper. We have an extra income tax just to help pay for this. It's called the Medicare levy (levy is just another word for tax).

We all have to pay the levy, BUT –
If you earn more than $90,000 per year, you'll have to pay *extra* unless you have good health insurance. That doesn't apply to most young adults.
That's called the Medicare Levy Surcharge.

So what does it mean for you?
Nothing, really. You can get health insurance if you choose to buy it for other reasons, but unless you earn more than that amount, it won't affect your tax.

After that, you're ready to lodge.
Too easy, right?

Tips and Tricks!

1) At the end of MyTax, you have the opportunity to print your tax return. DO THAT! Keep it with your other tax files.
2) Don't be afraid to call the ATO! Do it early in the morning, or you might be waiting for a long time on hold.
3) Use the ATO website! Don't just guess! It's a good website. Be patient, read slowly and carefully, and make notes.

Key Terms!

Superannuation	Money from your boss, kept in a bank account for you.
Super Contributions	Extra payments into your super! There can be some good benefits to this.
Interest	Money from your bank for storing your money with them.
Dividends	Small payments from shares (from that company's profits!).
Pre-fill	To take your information automatically from other records, and use it to complete parts of your tax return.
Sole Trader	A (usually small) business owner.
Medicare Levy	A tax to pay for healthcare.
Medicare Levy Surcharge	An extra tax for people with a strong income that don't buy health insurance.

Update from Hayden!

Hayden tried MyTax and liked it, but in the end he wanted some personal advice, so he went to a tax agent.

NO QUIZ FOR CHAPTER TWELVE!

Chapter Thirteen:
What is a Notice of Assessment?

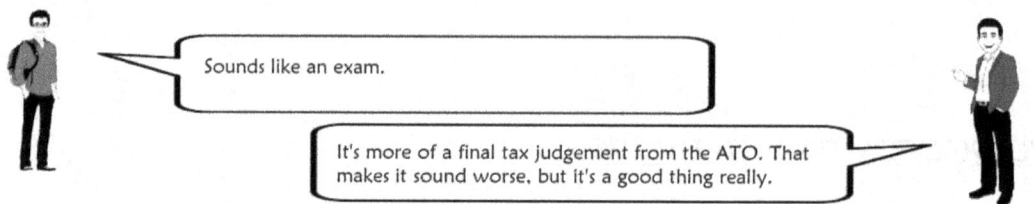

Sounds like an exam.

It's more of a final tax judgement from the ATO. That makes it sound worse, but it's a good thing really.

Why do I need this chapter?
This chapter explores the *what* and *why* of tax assessments.
1) What is a notice of assessment?
2) Why do I need it and what do I do with it?
3) How do I read it and what does it all mean?
4) What is a tax refund?
5) When can I expect my tax refund?
6) What if I think it's wrong? What is a tax amendment?

What is a Tax Assessment/Notice of Assessment?
A tax assessment is like a final tax judgement from the ATO. It tells you how much you earned, how much tax you were due to pay, and how much tax remains or will be refunded. It's usually the last document in the process.

What is a notice of assessment?
A notice of assessment is the same thing as a tax assessment.
It's a letter that you receive after you've lodged your tax return. When the ATO reads your tax return, they do a bunch of calculations to find out how much tax you were due to pay, and then they send you that summary in the form of your notice of assessment. It also tells you if you're receiving a tax refund or a bill.
Make sure you keep your assessment!

What is a tax refund?
Don't get confused:
Your tax return is the **paper form** you fill out.
Your tax refund is the **money** you get back.
If you've paid a lot of taxes during the year, you will get some money back. That's

your tax refund. If you haven't paid enough, you'll get a bill, and you'll have to pay it. Most individuals get a refund at the end of the year.

A tax refund is often paid directly into your bank account (as long as you provided them your bank details in your tax return).

It usually takes less than two weeks for you to receive your tax assessment and refund (if you get a one).

What if something's wrong? What is a tax amendment?
So, what if you receive your notice of assessment and realise that something doesn't seem right? Maybe your tax return was wrong, or some wrong calculation was made somewhere? Is it too late to try to change it?
You should talk to a tax agent or call the ATO. Depending on what it is, the ATO might issue a tax amendment. A tax amendment is a process when your tax return needs to be changed: the ATO redoes all the maths. Maybe that means you owe them money again, or maybe they owe you some. Tax amendments aren't all that common.

What do I do with my notice of assessment?
Nothing. Just keep it. It might come in handy later. And you're required to keep your records generally for five years. Why do you need it? It's a great summary and conclusion that shows how much tax you have to pay and why.

What does all this stuff on my notice of assessment mean?
Take a look at the example of a notice of assessment.
1) Your taxable income is the amount you earned during the year.
2) Any tax offsets/deductions (discounts).
3) How much tax you're due to pay.
4) How much you've already paid.
5) The difference: your refund or bill.

Tips and Tricks!
1) If this is your first tax assessment, sit with a parent and they might be able to show you what it means.
2) Check your bank account and make sure the money comes through!
3) Store your assessment carefully.

Mr So-and-So
Address here.

053

Tax period ending	30 June 2012
Tax file number	### ### ###
Date of issue	**15 August 2012**
Our reference	### ### ### ####

Internet: www.ato.gov.au Phone enquiries: 13 28 61

Notice of assessment - year ended 30 June 2012
Income Tax Assessment Act 1936 and Income Tax Assessment Act 1997

Description	Debits $	Credits $
Your taxable income is $ **Number 1**		
Tax on your taxable or net income		
Less non-refundable tax offsets		
Low income offset calculated by us		
Less refundable tax offsets		
Franking credit offset **Number 2**		
Assessed tax payable $ **Number 3**		
Plus other liabilities		
Medicare levy		
Less Pay as you go (PAYG) credits and other entitlements		
PAYG withholding (eg tax deducted by your employer or bank)		**Number 4**
Result of this notice		

Example Only

Outcome of this notice **Number 5**

⊘ Your refund of _____ has been forwarded to your nominated financial institution.

Please keep this notice for future reference
Deputy Commissioner of Taxation Please see over for important information about your assessment

Other information relevant to your assessment:
You did not pay the temporary flood and cyclone reconstruction levy because your taxable income is less than the threshold amount.

Update from Hayden!

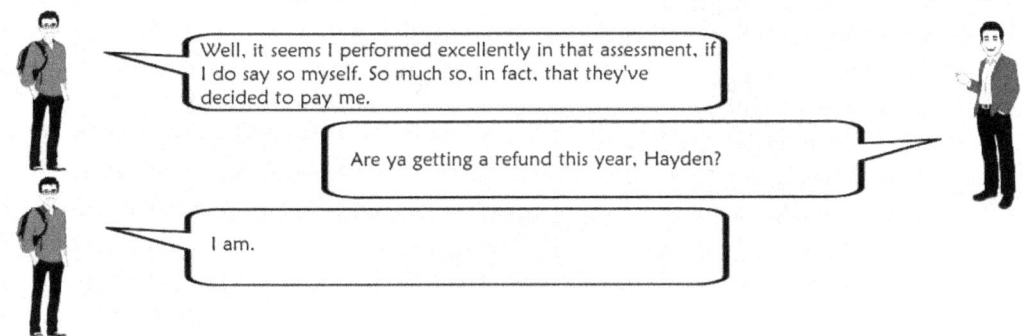

This year, Hayden was only working part-time. He was paying a small amount in tax withholding each pay cheque. In the end, he got a nice tax refund once he lodged his tax return. Good thing he remembered to lodge, or he wouldn't have received the money he was owed.

Hayden had a read through his tax assessment and put it in his folder with his other tax documents for that year.

Done.

Key Terms!

Notice of assessment	The result of your tax return, sent by the ATO.
Tax amendment	A change made to your tax return after lodgement, due to a mistake.
Tax refund	The money you get back if you've paid too much in tax.

CHAPTER THIRTEEN QUIZ TIME!
1. What is a tax assessment?
    a. The money you get back from the government for over-paid taxes.
    b. The tax return you prepare that assesses your tax situation.
    c. The government's judgement on your tax situation for the year past.
    d. Your tax agent's judgement on your tax situation for the year past.
2. Generally, how long are we supposed to keep our tax records?
    a. 1 Year.
    b. 5 years.
    c. Forever.
    d. We don't have to – the tax office does it once they have our tax return.
3. Why do we need a tax assessment?
    a. To prepare our tax returns.
    b. To prove our tax deductions are legitimate and not made-up.
    c. To assess whether or not to hire a tax agent.
    d. So that we can see in written form what the government has decided about our taxes for the year past.
4. What is a tax amendment?
    a. When something about your tax return was wrong and they need to do it again.
    b. The money you get back – amending you for over-paid taxes.
    c. A type of tax withholding – where you have to withhold more.
    d. Using the tax-agent to patch up your tax return before sending it to the ATO.
5. If you have questions about your tax assessment, you should:
    a. Talk to your tax agent.
    b. Call the ATO.
    c. Ask someone who might know, like a parent, or the ATO website.
    d. Any and all of the above.
6. Tax assessments are:
    a. Usually the last thing you receive from the tax office for that financial year.
    b. Usually the first thing you receive from the tax office for that financial year.
    c. Something you should complete as soon as you can.
    d. Only conducted if the government feels that you might be doing something wrong.
7. Some of the information you can find in your tax assessment is:

a. Who your tax agent is, how much your refund is, and how many times your boss withheld your taxes.
   b. Whether or not the tax office approved your return, or why your tax return has been refused.
   c. How much you earned, how much tax you've paid, and how much you owe or is owed to you.
   d. The income you earned in the financial year, and a request for a tax return.
8. When you receive your tax assessment you should:
   a. Read it over and check that the funds have come through into your account (if you are receiving a refund), then file it safely away in your organised tax file for future reference.
   b. Don't open the envelope. It's from the tax office and that's never good.
   c. Throw it away.

Chapter Fourteen:
How Can I Stay Organised?

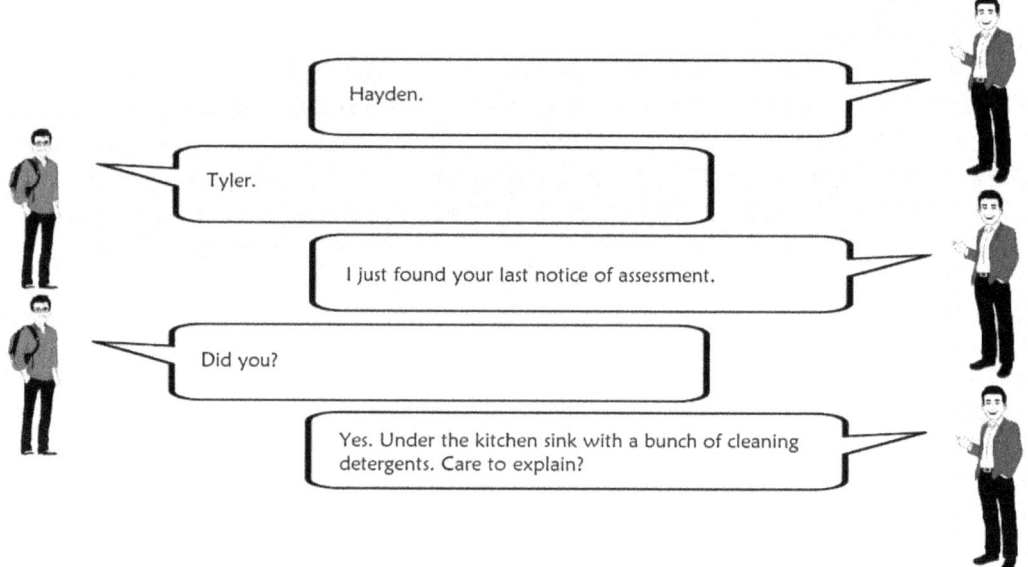

Why do I need this chapter?
This chapter explores the *how* of staying organised.
   1) What are my record-keeping obligations?
   2) Why must I keep records? For how long?
   3) What is an audit?
   4) Who can be audited and when?
   5) What could happen if they catch me lying?
   6) Which documents should I keep?
   7) What's the best way to keep documentation?
   8) How can I use organisation to save both time and money in the long term?

Why stay organised?
The ATO generally requires people to keep their documents for five years. It's best to keep your documents safe and organised in case you are audited.

What are my obligations? Why must I keep records?
The ATO has a policy of self-assessment, which means they're trusting that the information you give is correct (they won't check every individual tax return themselves to make sure!).

Instead of checking every little thing for every single person, they audit specific people (an audit is a check on your taxes). Sometimes it's random, sometimes there's a reason.

You are obligated to keep your records for between five years.
They can audit you in that time.

What is an audit?
An audit is a check. The government has the right to conduct random checks on people. They will also audit you if they have a suspicion that something might be wrong or false. When this happens, they can be very harsh and very thorough.

They will ask for the documentation that you were required to keep, and they will not accept excuses for not having those documents. If you are unable to prove something (a deduction was real, for example), even if you know it to be true, you might have to pay the extra tax.

Who can be audited and when?
Audits can be totally random, and can happen to anyone at any time.
But they can also be targeted. The will investigate you if they think something seems strange, like crazy amounts of deductions.

Which documents should I keep?
Any document that acts as a proof to help you pay less tax should be kept. These are some examples of documents that would be good to keep:
- A copy of your tax return.
- You receipts.
- Your notice of assessment.
- Your PAYG Payment Summaries.
- Interest statements from your bank.

What's the best way to store documents?
Get yourself a simple, effective filing system! Here's an example of one:
1) Get a folder or a file with different sections. Label each section with a year.
2) Put documents away according to the financial year of the document, and make notes on stuff that might confuse you later.
3) Put your file somewhere in your room or house where it's safe and won't get lost.

Simple, right?

For deductions:
When you buy something that could be claimed, put the receipt in a plastic sleeve with the other receipts as soon as you get home, and also write the deduction on a list like the one on the next page.

Some useful information you should write down when it comes to claiming deductions:
- What it is.
- When you got it.
- How much it was.
- Why you need it for work.

This way, when you sit down to do your taxes, your deductions will be easy. You could even just hand the file over to your tax agent and he'll do the whole thing.

Just make sure you *don't* put off doing your tax filing. File things away carefully *as soon as you get the receipt.*

What could happen if they catch me lying?
If you've been caught lying to save money on tax, they will make you repay the taxes with interest and probably make you pay a fine. People who are charged with tax fraud involving a lot of money, like inside a big company, can go to prison for it.

How can I be organised and save both time and money in the long term?
The biggest problem in putting off organisation is that people forget about and lose things. This can cost you in the end, in both money and time.

Use your filing system, be careful, be prudent, take good notes. Then you're fine!

Tips and Tricks!
1) Don't put things off!
2) Don't lose your folder!
3) Don't throw things out for five years at least.
4) Take good notes if you might forget something.

The hardest part of filing your tax paperwork is your receipts for deductions. People usually lose them. Some people run off one day and buy a pair of boots, they lose the receipt somewhere in their house or it goes in the wash, and then it never gets claimed.
Be organised!

List of Possible Tax Deductions for Financial Year: _____

This belongs to (Name): _____

Deduction	Cost	Where is the receipt?	Date bought:	Reason I Need It:
EXAMPLE Steel-Capped Boots	EXAMPLE $50	EXAMPLE In this tax folder.	EXAMPLE 8/11/2020	EXAMPLE Compulsory in the warehouse.

Update from Hayden!

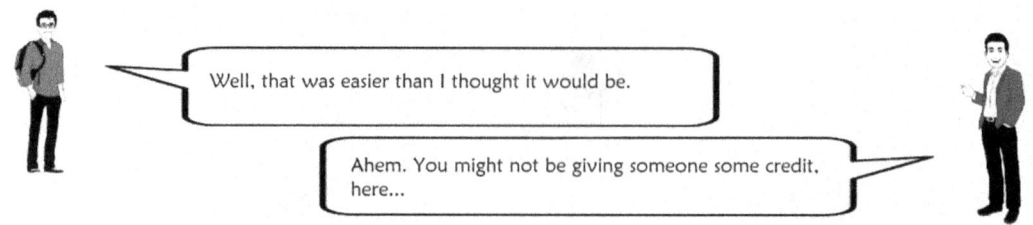

Big problems can be avoided with a simple filing system. Hayden got himself organised so he didn't have to worry or think. Once he had it sorted, he just put his documents away and moved on. He was always ready when something came up and he had to check some information.

Key terms!

Tax Audit — When the government checks on your past tax returns to see if there's anything wrong with them.

CHAPTER FOURTEEN QUIZ TIME!
1. The best thing to do with tax documents is:
    a. Create a simple but effective filing system to store them.
    b. Put them in a box all together and figure it out later.
    c. Chuck it all in the bin.
    d. Give them to your parents and put off having to file things yourself.
2. If you buy something for work that could be a deduction, the best thing to do is:
    a. Put the receipt in a box or plastic sleeve and send it to your boss.
    b. Write the details of the deduction into a list and put the receipt in a box or plastic sleeve.
    c. Keep all your receipts together and notify your tax agent as you receive them.
    d. Write out the information into a list and throw the receipt out (the ATO does not require you to keep the receipts themselves, only the information on them).
3. If you write a list of tax deductions, some information you should include is:
    a. What it is, how much it was, and a description of the item's appearance.
    b. How much it was, why you chose that brand and when you bought it.
    c. When you bought it, how much it was, what it is and why you needed it.
    d. What, when, and where you bought it, including a description of something good that happened that day.
4. The best way to file tax documents would be:
    a. By calendar year to make them easy to find.
    b. By financial year to make them easy to find and to keep them ordered by tax return.
    c. How long you worked that job.
    d. By how much money you got in your refund, because that's what matters most.
5. What is an audit?
    a. When the tax office takes you to court for lying on your tax return.
    b. When the tax office investigates your tax history to find errors and frauds.
    c. A document amending false and misleading tax returns.
    d. A small auditorium.
6. What happens when I get audited?
    a. The tax office will ask for and check over my tax records.

b. I will get charged with tax fraud.
  c. I will have to present the tax office with all my records and the records of my family.
  d. I have to call up the tax office. The process can always be done over the phone in about five minutes.
7. Staying organised is important because:
  a. Good habits make or break us – staying organised is a good way to stay in control of your life.
  b. Staying organised means less things will go wrong.
  c. Staying organised and informed is easier in the long run.
  d. All of the above.

Chapter Fifteen:
How Can I Save Money in Tax?

Why do I need this chapter?
This chapter explores the *how* of saving money.
1) What are the best ways to reduce my tax?
2) What's deductible and what isn't?
3) How does health insurance affect my tax?
4) What are tax offsets?
5) What are tax-free donations?
6) Does claiming the tax-free threshold save me money?

> This is general advice only: your tax agent is best placed to suggest the best tax-saving ideas for your situation.

What are the best ways to reduce my tax?
So, the bad news: the Australian government has restricted the potential for the ordinary young adult (with a simple return) to reduce their taxes, but you do have the tax-free threshold and deductions.

When your situation is more complex (home ownership, business ownership, trusts and company structures) there are more ideas on saving money in tax. Unfortunately, this book won't go into detail on those topics as they are simply too big and too complex, and this book tackles the basics.

See below the most common topics on reducing tax for a simple young adult's return.

Tax deductions: what's deductible and what isn't?
For information on what tax deductions are, see the tax deductions chapter of this book.

What can you claim?
You can claim things that you had to buy for work. There are strict rules about this. It's not always easy to know if you can deduct something. You can check with the ATO (website or call centre), or your tax accountant.

On the ATO site, there is information on this topic sorted by major occupations and industries. That helps.

Some common deductible things:
- Uniforms/clothes specifically for work
- Items used at work, like a resource book if you're a teacher, or a whistle if you're a sports coach.
- Boots for construction work.

Some common non-deductible things:
- Travel to and from work.
- Expenses accrued in searching for work.
- Your lunch you bought in your lunch break.

How Does Health Insurance Affect My Tax?
If you earn less than $90,000 each year, then it doesn't at all.

Everyone pays the **Medicare Levy**.
People who earn $90,000 or more without appropriate health insurance pay an extra levy called the **Medicare Levy Surcharge**.

If that's you, you might consider buying the appropriate level of health insurance to reduce your tax.

What are Tax Offsets?
Tax offsets are a reduction in the amount of tax you pay based on your personal circumstances. Here are some examples of tax offsets:
- The pensioners offset (when you're old)
- The carer's offset (when you care for someone disabled, for example)
- The overseas forces offset (when you're in the military and overseas)

Offsets are usually for specific and special circumstances, so they're not common with the ordinary employee. If you're uncertain, you could do your own research on each offset, or check with your tax agent!

Why are some donations tax-free?
Certain charitable organisations that are listed by the ATO can offer you an opportunity for a tax deduction. It's a good incentive for people to donate money to good causes. The way it works: If you give money to that charity, get a receipt. Then list that donation as an expense in your deductions. Now it's income-tax-free! But remember, it's not totally free, just tax-free.

Does Claiming the Tax-Free Threshold Save Me Money?
Do you remember the tax-free threshold? Your first $18,200 (it often changes) is tax-free. That amount is called the tax-free threshold.

So, does claiming it save me money?
It does in the short term, but it doesn't make a difference to your tax bill in the long term. Just about everyone is entitled to the tax-free threshold (people from other countries, for example, may or may not be entitled to it!). If you claim it, you're asking your boss to withhold less tax to account for the tax-free threshold, and telling him that the job is your main income.
With a second income (EG, a second job), you wouldn't claim it because then you'd be paying too little tax overall.

At the end of the financial year, the ATO and your accountant run the numbers. Whether you claim the threshold for a specific job or not, your tax payable for the year is the same.

Withholding tax is a little bit like paying back a friend you owe money to, except that the amount is a bit uncertain right now.
1) You could pay it all at once at the end of the year, when he comes asking (claiming the tax-free threshold for several jobs).
2) You could pay him a lot now, and get the extra back later (not claiming the tax free threshold for any job).
3) Or you could consistently pay him an amount that seems right (claiming the tax-free threshold for one job but not more).
This one is recommended.

Tips and Tricks!
1) Keep your receipts and claim your deductions.
2) Ask a tax agent if there are any tax offsets or other opportunities for tax savings that are appropriate for you!

Key Terms!

Public Hospital	A free hospital for all Australians.
Private Hospital	An expensive hospital not funded by tax money.
Health Insurance	Insurance that will pay for private medical help.
Tax Offset	A tax discount.
Tax-Exempt Donations	A donation that can be claimed as a deduction.

CHAPTER FIFTEEN QUIZ TIME!

1. Name as many ways as you can that a human theoretically can obtain any kind of tax benefit:

2. Tax Offsets...
    a. Are discounts for people who aren't Australian.
    b. Are discounts for people who complain about their taxes.
    c. Are discounts for people in a specific circumstance that is difficult.
    d. Are not discounts at all.
3. A good, safe way to save money is to...
    a. Claim deductions for stuff that is required for work and validated by the ATO.
    b. Buy lots and lots of stuff and claim it all as deductions.
    c. Claim things that aren't related to your job.
4. Which donations are tax-free?
    a. Any and all.
    b. Only the ones to organisations listed by the ATO.
    c. No donations.
    d. Only the ones to the government.
5. How can you find out if you are eligible for a tax offset? You can...
    a. Talk to a tax agent or research it yourself on the ATO website.
    b. Work out if you're earning enough money to live off.
    c. Check your payslips.
    d. All of the above.
6. Tax offsets are...
    a. Common for young people.
    b. Uncommon for young people.
    c. A terrible thing.

True or False:
7. I can claim the washing of certain work clothes as an expense.
8. I can claim travel expenses to and from work.
9. I can definitely get a tax benefit from any kind of health insurance.
10. We are all entitled to a tax offset.

Chapter Sixteen: Tax for Travellers

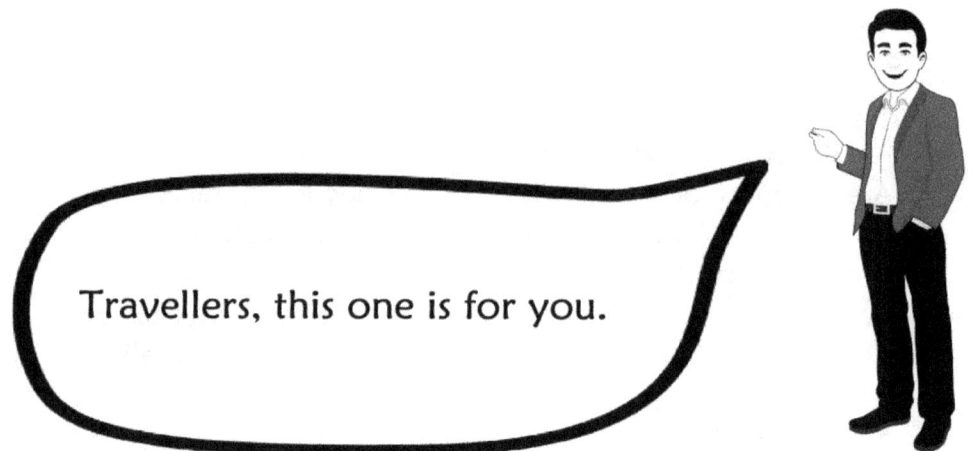

Travellers, this one is for you.

Why do I need this chapter?
This chapter explores the key differences in tax for someone from another country.
1) How does tax work between different countries?
2) Am I a resident for tax purposes?
3) What if I'm a resident?
4) What if not a resident?
5) Are the tax rates different for me?
6) And the tax-free threshold, is that different for me?
7) Is my tax "pro rata"?
8) What about my overseas assets and income?
9) What should I do when I leave Australia? What about my assets?

> Travellers in Australia may be subject to different tax rules compared to common Australian citizens. Those rules depend on many factors, including the length of stay and the visa granted.

We are heading into a murky, diverse, and complex area of taxes: international taxation. More than ever, *Mind the Gap* recommends you seek specialist advice in these areas.

This chapter contains general information only.
Tax and visa laws and policies change frequently.

What's a visa?
Some of you will already know exactly what a visa is.

A visa is a formal documented right, granted by a government to an individual, allowing them travel within the country of the visa. Think of it like a permission slip or a hall pass.

For example, the Australian government might grant someone from another country the right to come to Australia. The length of time and what they can and can't do in Australia depend on the type of visa.

There are many types of visas, including tourist visas (often short-term), working holiday visas (often medium-term), and permanent residency visas (often long-term).

A visa might go in your passport like a sticker or a stamp.
You often have to apply for you visa well before you leave your country, especially if it is a working visa.

How does tax work between different countries?
Every country has different laws in regards to overseas workers and overseas income. For example, some counties might require you to pay tax in your home country even if you live abroad. Others might not.

If you thought it was hard to understand one tax code, try understanding two tax codes and the each set of policies and laws that connects them.

In Australia, you're generally required to pay tax on your world-wide income if you're a resident for tax purposes (see more later in this chapter). That means that you'll have to pay tax on what you earn here as well as the income and assets you have overseas.

Am I a resident for tax purposes?

A resident for tax purposes is different to a permanent resident.

A permanent resident:
This is a person who has a long-term visa to live in Australia.
This is a visa-status.

A resident for tax purposes:

In essence, this is a person who lives and works in Australia and has made some form of home here.
This is a tax status.
People on many different types of visas can be a resident for tax purposes.

There are a few factors that influence whether or not you're a resident for tax purposes:
1) Your intention or purpose in Australia.
2) Your family, business and/or employment ties to Australia.
3) The location of your assets.
4) Your social and living arrangements.

So, how can you be sure for yourself?
The ATO website has a tool that will ask you questions about your situation, and tell you if you're a resident or not. Start there. If you're still not sure, call the ATO or ask a tax professional.

Below are some questions you might ask yourself:
1) Do you have a work visa and a TFN?
2) Are you working and living in a Australia?
3) For how long?
4) How often are you moving around?
1) Are you working various short-term jobs to get by, or one important one?
2) Did you leave most of your possessions in your home country, preparing for your return?

These influence your residency.
Your residency influences your tax rate (compare the differences below!).

So... think carefully about this situation. Your taxes might be lower if you're a resident. Do you fit into that category?

I'm a resident. What does that mean for me?
Firstly, Australia will tax you on your global income.
That's all incomes you receive while you're a resident, regardless of where the money comes from.

Secondly, Australia will generally tax you at a lower rate.
It may or may not be the same as an Australian citizen, however.

So, this may or may not be a good thing. If you own a lot of overseas assets, maybe you don't want to be a resident for tax purposes. If you don't own those assets, maybe you do want to be a resident.

And if I'm a non-resident. What would that mean for me?
Firstly, you would be taxed only on your Australian income, but it's a high rate. Secondly, you wouldn't have to pay the Medicare levy, but you wouldn't get access to Medicare benefits either.

Are the tax rates different for me, as a non-Australian?
They very well may be.

At the end of this book, you can see the tax bands for an ordinary Australian as at the time of publishing. Foreign residents and holiday makers each pay tax at different scales. These scales change, even yearly.

Other non-Australians might share the usual tax bands. That's very common.

Can I see the tax bands?
Here are the rates for working holiday makers (2017–18):

Taxable income	Tax on this income
$0–$37,000	15% on each $1 up to $37,000
$37,001–$87,000	32.5% on each $1 over $37,000 to $87,000
$87,001–$180,000	37% on each $1 over $87,000 to $180,000
$180,001 and over	45% on each $1 over $180,000

Here are the rates for foreign residents (2017–18):

Taxable income	Tax on this income
0 – $87,000	32.5c for each $1
$87,001 – $180,000	$28,275 plus 37c for each $1 over $87,000
$180,001 and over	$62,685 plus 45c for each $1 over $180,000

Note 1:
Be careful! These numbers change year to year, and only apply when a strict criteria has been fulfilled.

Note 2:
See the "$28,275 plus..."?
That's not an extra tax. That's a summary of the taxes from the previous bands. Example: $87,000 x 32.5% = $28,275. That's the tax payable on the money you earned below $87,000. For each dollar above, you pay the next rate.

And the tax-free threshold, is that different for me?
It might be, yes. See above.

Is my tax "pro rata"?
What's pro rata?
Look at this example:

Toby spent the whole financial year as a tax resident in Australia.
He earned $20,000. He paid taxes on $1,800 (because of the tax-free threshold).

Steve spent only half of the financial year as a tax resident in Australia. He spent the other half earning money overseas.
He also earned $20,000. Does he also pay tax on $1,800?
It doesn't seem fair. He was earning twice the income per week.

The answer is no. The tax rate would be adjusted for this difference.
That's pro rata: apportioning the tax rate more fairly.

What about my overseas assets and income?
They matter if you're a resident for tax purposes.
List that information in your tax return!
You may have to pay tax on them.

What should I do when I leave Australia? What about my assets?
Here are some things to remember when you're leaving Australia forever:
1) Take your superannuation with you.

Superannuation is money stored by your boss for your retirement. If you're not going to retire here in Australia, then you need to take that money, or it'll just rot away in a bank account. Talk to your superannuation provider.

2) Lodge your final tax return.

Many people are due a tax refund, and that doesn't change just because you're leaving Australia before the financial year has finished. Lodge your return!

3) Close your bank accounts properly and take the cash.

Open bank accounts with low funds or no funds can accumulate fees over time, into the negative even. Close your banks accounts!

Tips and Tricks!
1) Find out your tax residency – it's important or you could end up with a tax bill.
2) Take your assets with you when you leave Australia!

Key Terms!

Resident for tax Purposes	A person who lives and works in Australia generally for the longer-term.
Pro Rata	According to the time spent: apportioned fairly.
Overseas assets and incomes	Incomes and valuable things owned abroad.

CHAPTER SIXTEEN QUIZ TIME!

1) Can you take your superannuation with you when you leave?

2) Should you file a tax return if you were only in Australia for part of the year?

3) Is someone with a working visa automatically a tax resident?

4) Are residents for tax purposes generally taxed more or less?

5) Can every single person claim the tax-free threshold?

6) What should you remember to do when you leave Australia?

7) Does it matter if you earn money overseas?

8) What does pro rata mean?

9) Does everyone have the same tax bands?

Extra Information One: What are the tax rates?

The amount of tax you pay depends on how much you earn. The more you earn, the higher the percentage of tax you pay. This helps people on lower incomes who might find it hard to afford to live. The rate, or chart, that shows it is also called the tax bands. Take a look at the bands below:

0 – $18,200	Nil
$18,201 – $37,000	19c for each $1 over $18,200
$37,001 – $87,000	$3,572 plus 32.5c for each $1 over $37,000
$87,001 – $180,000	$19,822 plus 37c for each $1 over $87,000
$180,001 and over	$54,232 plus 45c for each $1 over $180,000

This chart is for the financial year 2017-2018. It can change each year!

You can see that over and above the tax-free threshold ($18,200 at the time of this book), employees must pay higher and higher rates of tax for each band that they enter.

Extra Information Two: What are some of the other taxes?

There are many taxes in the world. Below is an explanation of some of the taxes you might find in Australia.

INCOME TAX
This is the tax that this book was written about. It's the tax that workers pay on how much they earn.

GOODS AND SERVICES TAX
The Goods and Services Tax (The GST) is a tax on products or services you buy, for example a hairdryer, or a haircut. The current rate in Australia at the time of this book is 10%.

STAMP DUTY

This is a tax you have to pay when property (like a house or an apartment) is sold and bought. The government records the transfer of properties, and charges a tax on it.

THE MEDICARE LEVY

This is a tax that helps the government keep healthcare free to use (or cheaper). At this time, it's 2%, and almost all employees must pay it. You can avoid it in a few rare situations, the most likely situation being that you earn a very small income.

THE MEDICARE LEVY SURCHARGE

The *Medicare Levy Surcharge* is an *extra* Medicare tax, only for those who earn $90,000 every year and *don't* have an appropriate level of health insurance.

PROPERTY TAXES

These are taxes on owning many properties. If you own one house or apartment and live in it, you probably won't have to pay this tax. If you own more than one and rent it out, for example, the government taxes you.

CAPITAL GAINS TAX

If you buy a piece of art this year for $1000, and then sell it next year for $2000, you made a profit of $1000! Well done you! But that profit is income, so the government taxes you on it. When you pay taxes on something you profited from selling for more than you bought it for, it's called capital gains tax.

EXCISE TAXES

Some products have extra taxes. Two examples are alcohol and cigarettes. The government could tax a specific product like this to try to discourage people from using or overusing it.

That's it!

Want to see how much you've learnt? Below is the same quiz you took at the beginning of the book. Take it again now, and see how your score has improved!

Final Quiz!
1) PAYG Withholding Tax is:
    a. The method of paying income tax – "Pay as you go", or "pay as you earn".
    b. A type of income tax called "Payers Australia Yearly Gains".
    c. A category "G" Payment, where you take the money from your pay check and give it to the tax office every quarter.
    d. Payments that are held by the tax office, as a penalty for not paying taxes.
    e. A way to withhold tax from the government until you are ready to pay it.
2) You must complete your tax return:
    a. At the end of the calendar year.
    b. By Halloween.
    c. Just before the end of the financial year – the end of the financial year is the deadline.
    d. Just before the end of the calendar year – the end of the calendar year is the deadline.
    e. The ATO will inform you of your due date – it's different for each employee.
3) A tax file number is:
    a. The file at the tax office which holds the tax information for your family.
    b. A personal identifier – a number that identifies you to the Tax Office.
    c. The number allocated to each tax return as it is submitted (different for each tax return).
    d. All of the above
4) A good time to get your tax file number is:
    a. At least 30 days before you get your first job – it's impossible to work without a tax file number.
    b. You get your first job or before – as soon as you can (it's in your best interests).
    c. One floats down from the sky, because life is that easy.
    d. As late as you can, so you don't have to pay taxes for ages.
    e. Every person is automatically given a TFN.

5) A tax return is:
    a. When you have to return money to the government, because you didn't pay enough taxes.
    b. The amount of money the government returns to you for paying too much tax during the year.
    c. A form you fill out to help the tax office do a final tax count for the year just passed.
    d. The money you get when your tax assessment is returned to you.
    e. A document you fill out usually in December.
6) If you pay too much in withholding:
    a. You don't get it back.
    b. You should file a standard over-withholding form with the ATO to get your money back.
    c. You can't pay too much in withholding. The ATO is too careful and takes exactly the correct amount each time.
    d. It'll be returned to you when you lodge a tax return for that year.
    e. You have to file for a tax amendment.
7) An employee's income taxes are generally paid:
    a. By cash or card at any ATO shop front.
    b. By deducting the money directly from a person's pay.
    c. In the same way electricity or water bills are paid – a bill is sent.
    d. Whichever way of the above you choose to pay.
    e. At the end of the year with a tax return.
8) Forgetting to list a tax deduction will cause:
    a. You to get a smaller tax refund.
    b. You to pay more taxes throughout the year.
    c. You to get in trouble with the ATO, even fined.
    d. Nothing, tax deductions are withheld automatically.
9) What is a tax deduction?
    a. A reduction in the amount of tax you pay because of your living conditions.
    b. An expense – something you bought that you needed specifically for work. It means you pay less tax.
    c. The tax deducted from your pay check and sent to the ATO as withholding taxes.
    d. A voluntary payment of your taxes, paid as you buy something at a store, instead of paying the taxes through your employer.
10) A tax return is used by:
    a. The ATO, to produce a PAYG payment summary and therefore a potential refund.

b. Your boss, to pay your taxes to the ATO.
   c. The ATO, to produce a tax assessment and therefore a potential refund.
   d. You, it's the money you get back from the ATO.
   e. The ATO, because they can't give you your weekly wages without it.
11) What is a tax agent?
   a. Someone who organises your tax withholding.
   b. Someone who prepares your tax assessment.
   c. Someone who prepares your tax return.
   d. All of the above.

Answers!

1) A
2) B
3) B
4) B
5) C
6) D
7) B
8) A
9) B
10) C
11) C

Thank You!

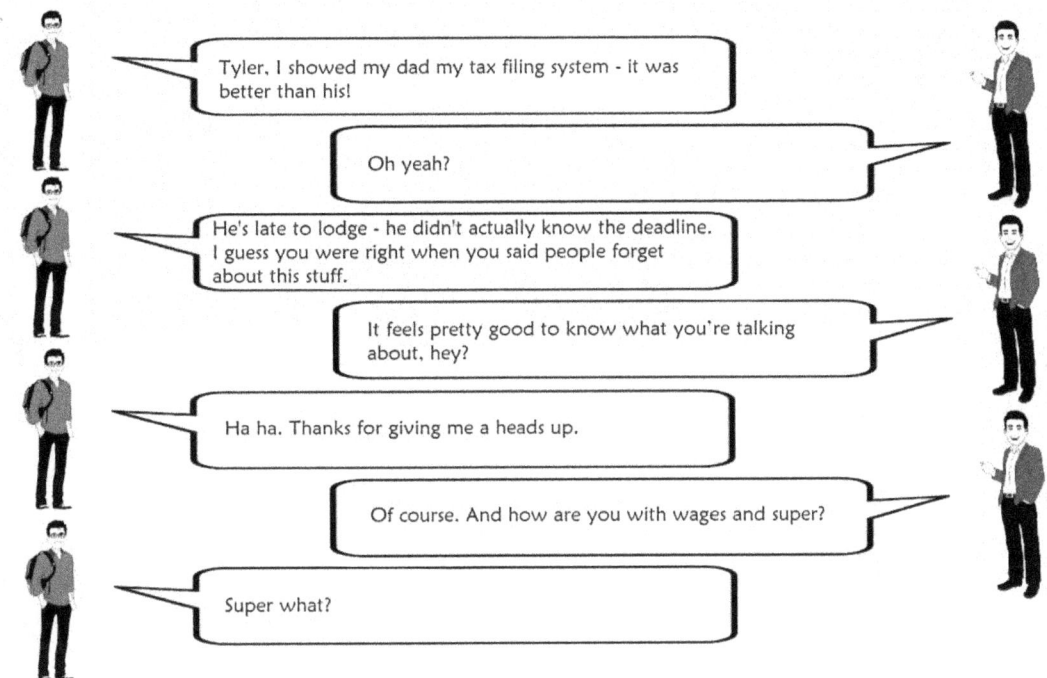

Keep an eye out for:

Mind the Gap: Your Job

Well done on completing an important tool; *Mind the Gap: Your Taxes*. You've learnt a lot and you're miles ahead of the pack. But! There *are* still some things you need to know.

Don't forget to pick up your next project: *Mind the Gap: Your Job.*
It's your handbook for the workplace:
- Superannuation
- Full-time, Part-time, Casual Work
- TFNs Vs. ABNs
- Modern Awards
- Benefits and Loadings
- Getting Help from Fair Work
- More!

It's everything you need to stay ahead of the pack and on track to your dreams!
Remember: it's your money, so you need to protect it.
No one else will.

Answers to the Quizzes:

QUIZ ONE:
1) C
2) E
3) A
4) D
5) F
6) B
7) A
8) A
9) D
10) C
11) A
12) A
13) C
14) A

QUIZ TWO:
1) Australian Tax Office
2) Call centre, website, fact sheets, videos.
3) To collect and administer taxes for the government.
4) A
5) B
6) D
7) B
8) A
9) C

QUIZ THREE:
1) July 1st to June 30th
2) -
3) A
4) A
5) B
6) B
7) C
8) B
9) A
10) B

QUIZ FOUR:
1) Y	8) Y	15) C
2) N	9) Y	16) D
3) Y	10) N	17) D
4) N	11) B	18) C
5) N	12) B	19) D
6) N	13) C	20) D
7) Y	14) B	

QUIZ FIVE:
1) B	8) F	15) C (B is a tax refund)
2) D	9) T	
3) C	10) T	16) A
4) A	11) F	17) A
5) F	12) T	18) B
6) T	13) T	19) B
7) F	14) F	

QUIZ SIX:
1) B	5) B
2) D	6) B
3) A	7) A
4) A	8) D

QUIZ SEVEN:
1) No	6) No
2) Yes	7) Yes
3) B	8) No
4) No	9) Yes
5) Yes	10) Yes

QUIZ EIGHT:
1) A
2) B
3) A
4) C
5) D
6) A
7) D
8) A

QUIZ NINE:
1) B
2) A
3) A
4) A
5) D
6) A
7) A
8) B
9) C
10) A

QUIZ TEN:
1) D
2) C
3) C
4) C
5) A
6) D
7) D

QUIZ ELEVEN:
1) C
2) B
3) A
4) D
5) A
6) A
7) C
8) A

QUIZ TWELVE:
NO QUIZ!

QUIZ THIRTEEN:
1) C
2) B
3) D
4) A
5) D
6) A
7) C
8) A

QUIZ FOURTEEN:
1) A
2) B
3) C
4) B
5) B
6) A
7) D

QUIZ FIFTEEN:
1) Deductions, donations, and sometimes health insurance and offsets. An accountant can also help.
2) C
3) A
4) B
5) A
6) B
7) T
8) F
9) F
10) F

QUIZ SIXTEEN:
1) Yes.
2) Yes.
3) No.
4) Less.
5) No.
6) File your taxes, close you bank accounts, take your super.
7) Yes, if you're a resident for tax purposes.
8) Apportioned for the amount of time.
9) No, not always.

Index of Terms

Accountant	A person whose job is working with financial numbers.
After-Tax Earnings	The money you get after taxes are taken out.
Allowances	This is money you get from your boss for extra expenses, like if they send you to a different city and give you some money for a hotel.
ATO	Australian Tax Office
ATO Fact Sheets	Information Sheets from the ATO about Different Topics
ATO Website	www.ato.gov.au
ATO Withholding Calculator	A program online from the ATO that calculates how much should be withheld from a person's pay.
Australia Post Website	www.auspost.com.au
Australian resident for tax purposes	Someone who lives in Australia and pays tax as a person living here.
Australian Tax Office	The government office for taxes.
Before tax earnings	The money you earn before taxes are taken out.
Benefits	Things you get from work that aren't money, but are valuable. For example, work might give you a car to use around the city.
Calendar Year	The normal calendar that we all use! January 1 to December 31 (as opposed to the financial year).
Casual	A type of employment with varying hours and less obligation.
Deduction	Money taken from your pay cheque for some reason. Maybe for a loan or child support or something. It's money that comes out of your pay cheque before you receive it.
File/Lodge	Both these words mean the same thing. They are verbs for when you give your return to the tax office.
Financial Year	The calendar for the business world: July 1 to June 30.
Full-time	Working 38ish hours per week.
Gross (payment)	Means total (payment), like before taxes.
Group Certificate	The same thing as your PAYG Summary.
GST	Goods and services tax, a tax on what you

	buy.
Health Insurance	Insurance that will pay for private medical help.
HELP and TSL Debts	University and studies debts.
Income tax	Tax on what we earn.
myGov	A government site that links a lot of your public services into one, like tax and welfare.
myTax	The government's program that you can use to lodge your return for free.
Notice of assessment	The result of your tax return, sent by the ATO.
Online tax agent	A tax agent from cyber space that you may never meet.
Part-time	Working fewer than 38ish hours per week.
Pay cheque	The money you receive for your work.
Payslip	A paper from your boss that explains your pay for this pay cycle.
PAYG payment summary	This is the summary your boss sends to you at the end of the financial year, so that you have the information you need to fill out your tax return.
PAYG tax	A name for the way we pay income tax: Pay As You Go.
Primary ID	Important ID, like your passport and driver's licence.
Private Hospital	An expensive hospital.
Public Hospital	A free hospital for all Australians.
Secondary ID	Slightly less important ID, like your Medicare card and bank statements.
Self-assessment	A policy from the government: the responsibility is yours to supply correct information, and you could get in trouble if you don't.
Stamp duty	A tax on selling a house.
Superannuation	Savings (from your boss) for when you're older.
Tax	Money to the government to pay for our country.
Tax Agent	An accountant that work with taxes and tax returns, and can help you lodge your tax return.
Tax amendment	A change in your tax, if there was a mistake realised after lodgement.
Tax Assessment	The letter from the ATO explaining how much tax you owe/get back.

Tax Audit	When the government checks on your past tax returns to see if there's anything wrong with them.
Tax Deduction	A tax discount because you spent money for your job.
Tax Evasion	Not paying your taxes.
Tax Help	A Free Tax Service for Low-Income Earners
Tax Offset	A tax discount.
Tax Rate	The percentages (or bands) of tax that a person pays on their income.
Tax Refund	The money you get back if you paid too much in taxes.
Tax Return	A document you provide to the ATO with your income information.
Tax Return Deadline	When your return is due! Halloween!
Tax Return Window	The four months you have to complete your return! July 1 – Oct 31.
Tax Withheld	Money taken to pay for your income tax.
Tax Withholding and Pay-As-You-Go	These are both terms to describe the way we pay income tax, which is a tax on what we earn.
Tax-Exempt Donations	A donation that can be claimed as a deduction.
TFN	Tax file number
Withholding Rate	The amount of money withheld from a pay check to pay for income tax.
Work-Related Expenses	This is similar to a tax deduction – usually they are the same thing. A work-related expense is the cost of buying something for work.

www.ingramcontent.com/pod-product-compliance
Lightning Source LLC
Chambersburg PA
CBHW080249170426
43192CB00014BA/2618